ISBN 0-8373-5341-6
41 COLLEGE LEVEL EXAMINATION SERIES/CLEP

CLEP

College-Level Examination Program
Subject Test In...

INTRODUCTORY MACRO-ECONOMICS

Test Preparation Study Guide

Questions and Answers

All rights reserved, including the right of reproduction in whole or in part, in any form or by any means, electronic or mechanical, including photocopying, recording, or by any information storage and retrieval system, without permission in writing from the Publisher.

Copyright © 2004 by

National Learning Corporation

212 Michael Drive, Syosset, New York 11791

(516) 921-8888
Outside N.Y.: 1(800) 645-6337
ORDER FAX: 1(516) 921-8743
www.passbooks.com
email: passbooks @ aol.com
sales @ passbooks.com
info @ passbooks.com

PRINTED IN THE UNITED STATES OF AMERICA

PASSBOOK®
NOTICE

This book is *SOLELY* intended for, is sold *ONLY* to, and its use is *RESTRICTED* to *individual*, bona fide applicants or candidates who qualify by virtue of having seriously filed applications for appropriate license, certificate, professional and/or promotional advancement, higher school matriculation, scholarship, or other legitimate requirements of educational and/or governmental authorities.

This book is *NOT* intended for use, class instruction, tutoring, training, duplication, copying, reprinting, excerption, or adaptation, etc., by:

(1) Other Publishers

(2) Proprietors and/or Instructors of "Coaching" and/or Preparatory Courses

(3) Personnel and/or Training Divisions of commercial, industrial, and governmental organizations

(4) Schools, colleges, or universities and/or their departments and staffs, including teachers and other personnel

(5) Testing Agencies or Bureaus

(6) Study groups which seek by the purchase of a single volume to copy and/or duplicate and/or adapt this material for use by the group as a whole without having purchased individual volumes for each of the members of the group

(7) Et al.

Such persons would be in violation of appropriate Federal and State statutes.

PROVISION OF LICENSING AGREEMENTS. — Recognized educational commercial, industrial, and governmental institutions and organizations, and others legitimately engaged in educational pursuits, including training, testing, and measurement activities, may address a request for a licensing agreement to the copyright owners, who will determine whether, and under what conditions, including fees and charges, the materials in this book may be used by them. In other words, a licensing facility *exists* for the legitimate use of the material in this book on other than an individual basis. However, it is asseverated and affirmed here that the materials in this book *CANNOT* be used without the receipt of the express permission of such a licensing agreement from the Publishers.

NATIONAL LEARNING CORPORATION
212 Michael Drive
Syosset, New York 11791

Inquiries re licensing agreements should be addressed to:
The President
National Learning Corporation
212 Michael Drive
Syosset, New York 11791

PASSBOOK SERIES®

THE *PASSBOOK SERIES*® has been created to prepare applicants and candidates for the ultimate academic battlefield—the examination room.

At some time in our lives, each and every one of us may be required to take an examination—for validation, matriculation, admission, qualification, registration, certification, or licensure.

Based on the assumption that every applicant or candidate has met the basic formal educational standards, has taken the required number of courses, and read the necessary texts, the *PASSBOOK SERIES*® furnishes the one special preparation which may assure passing with confidence, instead of failing with insecurity. Examination questions—together with answers—are furnished as the basic vehicle for study so that the mysteries of the examination and its compounding difficulties may be eliminated or diminished by a sure method.

This book is meant to help you pass your examination provided that you qualify and are serious in your objective.

The entire field is reviewed through the huge store of content information which is succinctly presented through a provocative and challenging approach—the question-and-answer method.

A climate of success is established by furnishing the correct answers at the end of each test.

You soon learn to recognize types of questions, forms of questions, and patterns of questioning. You may even begin to anticipate expected outcomes.

You perceive that many questions are repeated or adapted so that you gain acute insights, which may enable you to score many sure points.

You learn how to confront new questions, or types of questions, and to attack them confidently and work out the correct answers.

You note objectives and emphases, and recognize pitfalls and dangers, so that you may make positive educational adjustments.

Moreover, you are kept fully informed in relation to new concepts, methods, practices, and directions in the field.

You discover that you are actually taking the examination all the time: you are preparing for the examination by "taking" an examination, not by reading extraneous and/or supererogatory textbooks.

In short, this PASSBOOK®, used directedly, should be an important factor in helping you to pass your test.

College-Level Examination Program (CLEP)

1. WHAT IS CLEP?

CLEP stands for the College-Level Examination Program, sponsored by the College Board. It is a national program of credit-by-examination that offers you the opportunity to obtain recognition for college-level achievement. No matter when, where, or how you have learned – by means of formal or informal study – you can take CLEP tests. If the results are acceptable to your college, you can receive credit.

You may not realize it, but you probably know more than your academic record reveals. Each day you, like most people, have an opportunity to learn. In private industry and business, as well as at all levels of government, learning opportunities continually occur. If you read widely or intensively in a particular field, think about what you read, discuss it with your family and friends, you are learning. Or you may be learning on a more formal basis by taking a correspondence course, a television or radio course, a course recorded on tape or cassettes, a course assembled into programmed tests, or a course taught in your community adult school or high school.

No matter how, where, or when you gained your knowledge, you may have the opportunity to receive academic credit for your achievement that can be counted toward an undergraduate degree. The College-Level Examination Program (CLEP) enables colleges to evaluate your achievement and give you credit. A wide range of college-level examinations are offered by CLEP to anyone who wishes to take them. Scores on the tests are reported to you and, if you wish, to a college, employer, or individual.

2. WHAT ARE THE PURPOSES OF THE COLLEGE-LEVEL EXAMINATION PROGRAM?

The basic purpose of the College-Level Examination Program is to enable individuals who have acquired their education in nontraditional ways to demonstrate their academic achievement. It is also intended for use by those in higher education, business, industry, government, and other fields who need a reliable method of assessing a person's educational level.

Recognizing that the real issue is not how a person has acquired his education but what education he has, the College Level Examination Program has been designed to serve a variety of purposes. The basic purpose, as listed above, is to enable those who have reached the college level of education in nontraditional ways to assess the level of their achievement and to use the test results in seeking college credit or placement.

In addition, scores on the tests can be used to validate educational experience obtained at a nonaccredited institution or through noncredit college courses.

Some colleges and universities may use the tests to measure the level of educational achievement of their students, and for various institutional research purposes.

Other colleges and universities may wish to use the tests in the admission, placement, and guidance of students who wish to transfer from one institution to another.

Businesses, industries, governmental agencies, and professional groups now accept the results of these tests as a basis for advancement, eligibility for further training, or professional or semi-professional certification.

Many people are interested in the examination simply to assess their own educational progress and attainment.

The college, university, business, industry, or government agency that adopts the tests in the College-Level Examination Program makes its own decision about how it will use and interpret the test scores. The College Board will provide the tests, score them, and report the results either to the individuals who took the tests or the college or agency that administered them. It does NOT, and cannot, award college credit, certify college equivalency, or make recommendations regarding the standards these institutions should establish for the use of the test results.

Therefore, if you are taking the tests to secure credit from an institution, you should FIRST ascertain whether the college or agency involved will accept the scores. Each institution determines which CLEP tests it will accept for credit and the amount of credit it will award. If you want to take tests for college credit, first call, write, or visit the college you wish to attend to inquire about its policy on CLEP scores, as well as its other admission requirements.

The services of the program are also available to people who have been requested to take the tests by an employer, a professional licensing agency, a certifying agency, or by other groups that recognize college equivalency on the basis of satisfactory CLEP scores. You may, of course, take the tests SOLELY for your own information. If you do, your scores will be reported only to you.

While neither CLEP nor the College Board can evaluate previous credentials or award college credit, you will receive, with your scores, basic information to help you interpret your performance on the tests you have taken.

3. WHAT ARE THE COLLEGE-LEVEL EXAMINATIONS?

In order to meet different kinds of curricular organization and testing needs at colleges and universities, the College-Level Examination Program offers 35 different subject tests falling under five separate general categories: Composition and Literature, Foreign Languages, History and Social Sciences, Science and Mathematics, and Business.

4. WHAT ARE THE SUBJECT EXAMINATIONS?

The 35 CLEP tests offered by the College Board are listed below:

COMPOSITION AND LITERATURE:
- American Literature
- Analyzing and Interpreting Literature
- English Composition
- English Composition with Essay
- English Literature
- Freshman College Composition
- Humanities

FOREIGN LANGUAGES
- French
- German
- Spanish

HISTORY AND SOCIAL SCIENCES
- American Government
- Introduction to Educational Psychology
- History of the United States I: Early Colonization to 1877
- History of the United States II: 1865 to the Present
- Human Growth and Development
- Principles of Macroeconomics
- Principles of Microeconomics
- Introductory Psychology
- Social Sciences and History
- Introductory Sociology
- Western Civilization I: Ancient Near East to 1648
- Western Civilization II: 1648 to the Present

SCIENCE AND MATHEMATICS
- College Algebra
- College Algebra-Trigonometry
- Biology
- Calculus
- Chemistry
- College Mathematics
- Natural Sciences
- Trigonometry
- Precalculus (*available 2006)

BUSINESS
- Principles of Accounting
- Introductory Business Law
- Information Systems and Computer Applications
- Principles of Management
- Principles of Marketing

CLEP Examinations cover material taught in courses that most students take as requirements in the first two years of college. A college usually grants the same amount of credit to students earning satisfactory scores on the CLEP examination as it grants to students successfully completing the equivalent course.

Many examinations are designed to correspond to one-semester courses; some, however, correspond to full-year or two-year courses.

Each exam is 90 minutes long and, except for English Composition with Essay, is made up primarily of multiple-choice questions. Some tests have several other types of questions besides multiple choice. To see a more detailed description of a particular CLEP exam, visit www.collegeboard.com/clep.

The English Composition with Essay exam is the only exam that includes a required essay. This essay is scored by college English faculty designated by CLEP and does not require an additional fee. However, other Composition and Literature tests offer optional essays, which some college and universities require and some do not. These essays are graded by faculty at the individual institutions that require them and require an additional $10 fee. Contact the particular institution to ask about essay requirements, and check with your test center for further details.

All 35 CLEP examinations are administered on computer. If you are unfamiliar with taking a test on a computer, consult the CLEP Sampler online at www.collegeboard.com/clep. The Sampler contains the same tutorials as the actual exams and helps familiarize you with navigation and how to answer different types of questions.

Points are not deducted for wrong or skipped answers – you receive one point for every correct answer. Therefore it is best that an answer is supplied for each exam question, whether it is a guess or not. The number of correct answers is then converted to a formula score. This formula, or "scaled," score is determined by a statistical process called *equating*, which adjusts for slight differences in difficulty between test forms and ensures that your score does not depend on the specific test form you took or how well others did on the same form. The scaled scores range from 20 to 80 – this is the number that will appear on your score report.

To ensure that you complete all questions in the time allotted, you would probably be wise to skip the more difficult or perplexing questions and return to them later. Although the multiple-choice items in these tests are carefully designed so as not to be tricky, misleading, or ambiguous, on the other hand, they are not all direct questions of factual information. They attempt, in their way, to elicit a response that indicates your knowledge or lack of knowledge of the material in question or your ability or inability to use or interpret a fact or idea. Thus, you should concentrate on answering the questions as they appear to be without attempting to out guess the testmakers.

5. WHAT ARE THE FEES?

The fee for all CLEP examinations is $55. Optional essays required by some institutions are an additional $10.

6. WHEN ARE THE TESTS GIVEN?

CLEP tests are administered year-round. Consult the CLEP website (www.collegeboard.com/clep) and individual test centers for specific information.

7. WHERE ARE THE TESTS GIVEN?

More than 1,300 test centers are located on college and university campuses throughout the country, and additional centers are being established to meet increased needs. Any accredited collegiate institution with an explicit and publicly available policy of credit by examination can become a CLEP test center. To obtain a list of these centers, visit the CLEP website at www.collegeboard.com/clep.

8. HOW DO I REGISTER FOR THE COLLEGE-LEVEL EXAMINATION PROGRAM?

Contact an individual test center for information regarding registration, scheduling and fees. Registration/admission forms can also be obtained on the CLEP website.

9. MAY I REPEAT THE COLLEGE-LEVEL EXAMINATIONS?

You may repeat any examination providing at least six months have passed since you were last administered this test. If you repeat a test within a period of time less than six months, your scores will be cancelled and your fees forfeited. To repeat a test, check the appropriate space on the registration form.

10. WHEN MAY I EXPECT MY SCORE REPORTS?

With the exception of the English Composition with Essay exam, you should receive your score report instantly once the test is complete.

11. HOW SHOULD I PREPARE FOR THE COLLEGE-LEVEL EXAMINATIONS?

This book has been specifically designed to prepare candidates for these examinations. It will help you to consider, study, and review important content, principles, practices, procedures, problems, and techniques in the form of varied and concrete applications.

12. QUESTIONS AND ANSWERS APPEARING IN THIS PUBLICATION

The College-Level Examinations are offered by the College Board. Since copies of past examinations have not been made available, we have used equivalent materials, including questions and answers, which are highly recommended by us as an appropriate means of preparing for these examinations.

If you need additional information about CLEP Examinations, visit www.collegeboard.com/clep.

THE COLLEGE-LEVEL EXAMINATION PROGRAM

How The Program Works

CLEP examinations are administered at many colleges and universities across the country, and most institutions award college credit to those who do well on them. The examinations provide people who have acquired knowledge outside the usual educational settings the opportunity to show that they have learned college-level material without taking certain college courses.

The CLEP examinations cover material that is taught in introductory-level courses at many colleges and universities. Faculties at individual colleges review the tests to ensure that they cover the important material taught in their courses. Colleges differ in the examinations they accept; some colleges accept only two or three of the examinations while others accept nearly all of them.

Although CLEP is sponsored by the College Board and the examinations are scored by Educational Testing Service (ETS), neither of these organizations can award college credit. Only accredited colleges may grant credit toward a degree. When you take a CLEP examination, you may request that a copy of your score report be sent to the college you are attending or plan to attend. After evaluating your scores, the college will decide whether or not to award you credit for a certain course or courses, or to exempt you from them. If the college gives you credit, it will record the number of credits on your permanent record, thereby indicating that you have completed work equivalent to a course in that subject. If the college decides to grant exemption without giving you credit for a course, you will be permitted to omit a course that would normally be required of you and to take a course of your choice instead.

What the Examinations Are Like

The examinations consist mostly of multiple-choice questions to be answered within a 90-minute time limit. Additional information about each CLEP examination is given in the examination guide and on the CLEP website.

Where To Take the Examinations

CLEP examinations are administered throughout the year at the test centers of approximately 1,300 colleges and universities. On the CLEP website, you will find a list of institutions that award credit for satisfactory scores on CLEP examinations. Some colleges administer CLEP examinations to their own students only. Other institutions administer the tests to anyone who registers to take them. If your college does not administer the tests, contact the test centers in your area for information about its testing schedule.

Once you have been tested, your score report will be available instantly. CLEP scores are kept on file at ETS for 20 years; and during this period, for a small fee, you may have your transcript sent to another college or to anyone else you specify. (Your scores will never be sent to anyone without your approval.)

APPROACHING A COLLEGE ABOUT CLEP

The following sections provide a step-by-step approach to learning about the CLEP policy at a particular college or university. The person or office that can best assist students desiring CLEP credit may have a different title at each institution, but the following guidelines will lead you to information about CLEP at any institution.

Adults returning to college often benefit from special assistance when they approach a college. Opportunities for adults to return to formal learning in the classroom are now widespread, and colleges and universities have worked hard to make this a smooth process for older students. Many colleges have established special service offices that are staffed with trained professionals who understand the kinds of problems facing adults returning to college. If you think you might benefit from such assistance, be sure to find out whether these services are available at your college.

How to Apply for College Credit

STEP 1. Obtain the General Information Catalog and a copy of the CLEP policy from the colleges you are considering. If you have not yet applied for admission, ask for an admissions application form too.

Information about admissions and CLEP policies can be obtained by contacting college admissions offices or finding admissions information on the school websites. Tell the admissions officer that you are a prospective student and that you are interested in applying for admission and CLEP credit. Ask for a copy of the publication in which the college's complete CLEP policy is explained. Also get the name and the telephone number of the person to contact in case you have further questions about CLEP.

At this step, you may wish to obtain information from external degree colleges. Many adults find that such colleges suit their needs exceptionally well.

STEP 2. If you have not already been admitted to the college you are considering, look at its admission requirements for undergraduate students to see if you can qualify.

This is an important step because if you can't get into college, you can't get college credit for CLEP. Nearly all colleges require students to be admitted and to enroll in one or more courses before granting the students CLEP credit.

Virtually all public community colleges and a number of four-year state colleges have open admission policies for in-state students. This usually means that they admit anyone who has graduated from high school or has earned a high school equivalency diploma.

If you think you do not meet the admission requirements, contact the admissions office for an interview with a counselor. Colleges do sometimes make exceptions, particularly for adult applicants. State why you want the interview and ask what documents you should bring with you or send in advance. (These materials may include a high school transcript, transcript of previous college work, completed application for admission, etc.) Make an extra effort to have all the information requested in time for the interview.

During the interview, relax and be yourself. Be prepared to state honestly why you think you are ready and able to do college work. If you have already taken CLEP examinations and scored high enough to earn credit, you have shown that you are able to do college work. Mention this achievement to the admissions counselor because it may increase your chances of being accepted. If you have not taken a CLEP examination, you can still improve your chances of being accepted by describing how your job training or independent study has helped prepare you for college-level work. Tell the counselor what you have learned from your work and personal experiences.

STEP 3. Evaluate the college's CLEP policy.

Typically, a college lists all its academic policies, including CLEP policies, in its general catalog. You will probably find the CLEP policy statement under a heading such as Credit-by-Examination, Advanced Standing, Advanced Placement, or External Degree Program. These sections can usually be found in the front of the catalog.

Many colleges publish their credit-by-examination policies in a separate brochure, which is distributed through the campus testing office, counseling center, admissions office, or registrar's office. If you find a very general policy statement in the college catalog, seek clarification from one of these offices.

Review the material in the section of this guide entitled Questions to Ask About a College's CLEP Policy. Use these guidelines to evaluate the college's CLEP policy. If you have not yet taken a CLEP examination, this evaluation will help you decide which examinations to take and whether or not to take the free-response or essay portion. Because individual colleges have different CLEP policies, a review of several policies may help you decide which college to attend.

STEP 4. If you have not yet applied for admission, do so early.

Most colleges expect you to apply for admission several months before you enroll, and it is essential that you meet the published application deadlines. It takes time to process your application for admission; and if you have yet to take a CLEP examination, it will be some time before the college receives and reviews your score report. You will probably want to take some, if not all, of the CLEP examinations you are interested in before you enroll so you know which courses you need not register for. In fact, some colleges require that all CLEP scores be submitted before a student registers.

Complete all forms and include all documents requested with your application(s) for admission. Normally, an admissions decision cannot be reached until all documents have been submitted and evaluated. Unless told to do so, do not send your CLEP scores until you have been officially admitted.

STEP 5. Arrange to take CLEP examination(s) or to submit your CLEP score(s).

You may want to wait to take your CLEP examinations until you know definitely which college you will be attending. Then you can make sure you are taking tests your college will accept for credit. You will also be able to request that your scores be sent to the college, free of charge, when you take the tests.

If you have already taken CLEP examinations, but did not have a copy of your score report sent to your college, you may request the College Board to send an official transcript at any time for a small fee. Use the Transcript Request Form that was sent to you with your score report. If you do not have the form, you may find it online at www.collegeboard.com/clep.

Your CLEP scores will be evaluated, probably by someone in the admissions office, and sent to the registrar's office to be posted on your permanent record once you are enrolled. Procedures vary from college to college, but the process usually begins in the admissions office.

STEP 6. Ask to receive a written notice of the credit you receive for your CLEP score(s).

A written notice may save you problems later, when you submit your degree plan or file for graduation. In the event that there is a question about whether or not you earned CLEP credit, you will have an official record of what credit was awarded. You may also need this verification of course credit if you go for academic counseling before the credit is posted on your permanent record.

STEP 7. Before you register for courses, seek academic counseling.

A discussion with your academic advisor can prevent you from taking unnecessary courses and can tell you specifically what your CLEP credit will mean to you. This step may be accomplished at the time you enroll. Most colleges have orientation sessions for new students prior to each enrollment period. During orientation, students are usually assigned an academic advisor who then gives them individual help in developing long-range plans and a course schedule for the next semester. In conjunction with this counseling, you may be asked to take some additional tests so that you can be placed at the proper course level.

External Degree Programs

If you have acquired a considerable amount of college-level knowledge through job experience, reading, or noncredit courses, if you have accumulated college credits at a variety of colleges over a period of years, or if you prefer studying on your own rather than in a classroom setting, you may want to investigate the possibility of enrolling in an external degree program. Many colleges offer external degree programs that allow you to earn a degree by passing examinations (including CLEP), transferring credit from other colleges, and demonstrating in other ways that you have satisfied the educational requirements. No classroom attendance is required, and the programs are open to out-of-state candidates as well as residents. Thomas A. Edison State College in New Jersey and Charter Oaks College in Connecticut are fully accredited independent state colleges; the New York program is part of the state university system and is also fully accredited. If you are interested in exploring an external degree, you can write for more information to:

Charter Oak College
The Exchange, Suite 171
270 Farmington Avenue
Farmington, CT 06032-1909

Regents External Degree Program
Cultural Education Center
Empire State Plaza
Albany, New York 12230

Thomas A. Edison State College
101 West State Street
Trenton, New Jersey 08608

Many other colleges also have external degree or weekend programs. While they often require that a number of courses be taken on campus, the external degree programs tend to be more flexible in transferring credit, granting credit-by-examination, and allowing independent study than other traditional programs. When applying to a college, you may wish to ask whether it has an external degree or weekend program.

Questions to Ask About a College's CLEP Policy

Before taking CLEP examinations for the purpose of earning college credit, try to find the answers to these questions:

1. Which CLEP examinations are accepted by this college?

A college may accept some CLEP examinations for credit and not others - possibly not the one you are considering. The English faculty may decide to grant college English credit based on the CLEP English Composition examination, but not on the Freshman College Composition examination. Or, the mathematics faculty may decide to grant credit based on the College Mathematics to non-mathematics majors only, requiring majors to take an examination in algebra, trigonometry, or calculus to earn credit. For these reasons, it is important that you know the specific CLEP tests for which you can receive credit.

2. Does the college require the optional free-response (essay) section as well as the objective portion of the CLEP examination you are considering?

Knowing the answer to this question ahead of time will permit you to schedule the optional essay examination when you register to take your CLEP examination.

3. Is credit granted for specific courses? If so, which ones?

You are likely to find that credit will be granted for specific courses and the course titles will be designated in the college's CLEP policy. It is not necessary, however, that credit be granted for a specific course in order for you to benefit from your CLEP credit. For instance, at many liberal arts colleges, all students must take certain types of courses; these courses may be labeled the core curriculum, general education requirements, distribution requirements, or liberal arts requirements. The requirements are often expressed in terms of credit hours. For example, all students may be required to take at least six hours of humanities, six hours of English, three hours of mathematics, six hours of natural science, and six hours of social science, with no particular courses in these disciplines specified. In these instances, CLEP credit may be given as 6 hrs. English credit or 3 hrs. Math credit without specifying for which English or mathematics courses credit has been awarded. In order to avoid possible disappointment, you should know before taking a CLEP examination what type of credit you can receive and whether you will only be exempted from a required course but receive no credit.

4. How much credit is granted for each examination you are considering, and does the college place a limit on the total amount of CLEP credit you can earn toward your degree?

Not all colleges that grant CLEP credit award the same amount for individual tests. Furthermore, some colleges place a limit on the total amount of credit you can earn through CLEP or other examinations. Other colleges may grant you exemption but no credit toward your degree. Knowing several colleges' policies concerning these issues may help you decide which college you will attend. If you think you are capable of passing a number of CLEP examinations, you may want to attend a college that will allow you to earn credit for all or most of them. For example, the state external degree programs grant credit for most CLEP examinations (and other tests as well).

5. What is the required score for earning CLEP credit for each test you are considering?

Most colleges publish the required scores or percentile ranks for earning CLEP credit in their general catalog or in a brochure. The required score may vary from test to test, so find out the required score for each test you are considering.

6. What is the college's policy regarding prior course work in the subject in which you are considering taking a CLEP test?

Some colleges will not grant credit for a CLEP test if the student has already attempted a college-level course closely aligned with that test. For example, if you successfully completed English 101 or a comparable course on another campus, you will probably not be permitted to receive CLEP credit in that subject, too. Some colleges will not permit you to earn CLEP credit for a course that you failed.

7. Does the college make additional stipulations before credit will be granted?

It is common practice for colleges to award CLEP credit only to their enrolled students. There are other stipulations, however, that vary from college to college. For example, does the college require you to formally apply for or accept CLEP credit by completing and signing a form? Or does the college require you to validate your CLEP score by successfully completing a more advanced course in the subject? Answers to these and other questions will help to smooth the process of earning college credit through CLEP.

The above questions and the discussions that follow them indicate some of the ways in which colleges' CLEP policies can vary. Find out as much as possible about the CLEP policies at the colleges you are interested in so you can choose a college with a policy that is compatible with your educational goals. Once you have selected the college you will attend, you can find out which CLEP examinations your college recognizes and the requirements for earning CLEP credit.

DECIDING WHICH EXAMINATIONS TO TAKE

If You're Taking the Examinations for College Credit or Career Advancement:

Most people who take CLEP examinations do so in order to earn credit for college courses. Others take the examinations in order to qualify for job promotions or for professional certification or licensing. It is vital to most candidates who are taking the tests for any of these reasons that they be well prepared for the tests they are taking so that they can advance as rapidly as possible toward their educational or career goals.

It is usually advisable that those who have limited knowledge in the subjects covered by the tests they are considering enroll in the college courses in which that material is taught. Those who are uncertain about whether or not they know enough about a subject to do well on a particular CLEP test will find the following guidelines helpful.

There is no way to predict if you will pass a particular CLEP examination, but answers to the questions under the seven headings below should give you an indication of whether or not you are likely to succeed.

1. Test Descriptions

Read the description of the test provided. Are you familiar with most of the topics and terminology in the outline?

2. Textbooks

Examine the suggested textbooks and other resource materials following the test descriptions in this guide. Have you recently read one or more of these books, or have you read similar college-level books on this subject? If you have not, read through one or more of the textbooks listed, or through the textbook used for this course at your college. Are you familiar with most of the topics and terminology in the book?

3. Sample Questions

The sample questions provided are intended to be typical of the content and difficulty of the questions on the test. Although they are not an exact miniature of the test, the proportion of the sample questions you can answer correctly should be a rough estimate of the proportion of questions you will be able to answer correctly on the test.

Answer as many of the sample questions for this test as you can. Check your answers against the correct answers. Did you answer more than half the questions correctly?

Because of variations in course content at different institutions, and because questions on CLEP tests vary from easy to difficult - with most being of moderate difficulty - the average student who passes a course in a subject can usually answer correctly about half the questions on the corresponding CLEP examination. Most colleges set their passing scores near this level, but some set them higher. If your college has set its required score above the level required by most colleges, you may need to answer a larger proportion of questions on the test correctly.

4. Previous Study

Have you taken noncredit courses in this subject offered by an adult school or a private school, through correspondence, or in connection with your job? Did you do exceptionally well in this subject in high school, or did you take an honors course in this subject?

5. Experience

Have you learned or used the knowledge or skills included in this test in your job or life experience? For example, if you lived in a Spanish-speaking country and spoke the language for a year or more, you might consider taking the Spanish examination. Or, if you have worked at a job in which you used accounting and finance skills, Principles of Accounting would be a likely test for you to take. Or, if you have read a considerable amount of literature and attended many art exhibits, concerts, and plays, you might expect to do well on the Humanities exam.

6. Other Examinations

Have you done well on other standardized tests in subjects related to the one you want to take? For example, did you score well above average on a portion of a college entrance examination covering similar skills, or did you obtain an exceptionally high score on a high school equivalency test or a licensing examination in this subject? Although such tests do not cover exactly the same material as the CLEP examinations and may be easier, persons who do well on these tests often do well on CLEP examinations, too.

7. Advice

Has a college counselor, professor, or some other professional person familiar with your ability advised you to take a CLEP examination?

If your answer was yes to questions under several of the above headings, you probably have a good chance of passing the CLEP examination you are considering. It is unlikely that you would have acquired sufficient background from experience alone. Learning gained through reading and study is essential, and you will probably find some additional study helpful before taking a CLEP examination.

If You're Taking the Examinations to Prepare for College

Many people entering college, particularly adults returning to college after several years away from formal education, are uncertain about their ability to compete with other college students. They wonder whether they have sufficient background for college study, and those who have been away from formal study for some time wonder whether they have forgotten how to study, how to take tests, and how to write papers. Such people may wish to improve their test-taking and study skills prior to enrolling in courses.

One way to assess your ability to perform at the college level and to improve your test-taking and study skills at the same time is to prepare for and take one or more CLEP examinations. You need not be enrolled in a college to take a CLEP examination, and you may have your scores sent only to yourself and later request that a transcript be sent to a college if you then decide to apply for credit. By reviewing the test descriptions and sample questions, you may find one or several subject areas in which you think you have substantial knowledge. Select one examination, or more if you like, and carefully read at least one of the textbooks listed in the bibliography for the test. By doing this, you will get a better idea of how much you know of what is usually taught in a college-level course in that subject. Study as much material as you can, until you think you have a good grasp of the subject matter. Then take the test at a college in your area. It will be several weeks before you receive your results, and you may wish to begin reviewing for another test in the meantime.

To find out if you are eligible for credit for your CLEP score, you must compare your score with the score required by the college you plan to attend. If you are not yet sure which college you will attend, or whether you will enroll in college at all, you should begin to follow the steps outlined. It is best that you do this before taking a CLEP test, but if you are taking the test only for the experience and to familiarize yourself with college-level material and requirements, you might take the test before you approach a college. Even if the college you decide to attend does not accept the test you took, the experience of taking such a test will enable you to meet with greater confidence the requirements of courses you will take.

You will find information about how to interpret your scores in WHAT YOUR SCORES MEAN, which you will receive with your score report, and which can also be found online at the CLEP website. Many colleges follow the recommendations of the American Council on Education (ACE) for setting their required scores, so you can use this information as a guide in determining how well you did. The ACE recommendations are included in the booklet.

If you do not do well enough on the test to earn college credit, don't be discouraged. Usually, it is the best college students who are exempted from courses or receive credit-by-examination. The fact that you cannot get credit for your score means that you should probably enroll in a college course to learn the material. However, if your score was close to the required score, or if you feel you could do better on a second try or after some additional study, you may retake the test after six months. Do not take it sooner or your score will not be reported and your fee will be forfeited.

If you do earn the score required to earn credit, you will have demonstrated that you already have some college-level knowledge. You will also have a better idea whether you should take additional CLEP examinations. And, what is most important, you can enroll in college with confidence, knowing that you do have the ability to succeed.

PREPARING TO TAKE CLEP EXAMINATIONS

Having made the decision to take one or more CLEP examinations, most people then want to know if it is worthwhile to prepare for them - how much, how long, when, and how should they go about it? The precise answers to these questions vary greatly from individual to individual. However, most candidates find that some type of test preparation is helpful.

Most people who take CLEP examinations do so to show that they have already learned the important material that is taught in a college course. Many of them need only a quick review to assure themselves that they have not forgotten some of what they once studied, and to fill in some of the gaps in their knowledge of the subject. Others feel that they need a thorough review and spend several weeks studying for a test. A few wish to take a CLEP examination as a kind of final examination for independent study of a subject instead of the college course. This last group requires significantly more study than those who only need to review, and they may need some guidance from professors of the subjects they are studying.

The key to how you prepare for CLEP examinations often lies in locating those skills and areas of prior learning in which you are strong and deciding where to focus your energies. Some people may know a great deal about a certain subject area, but may not test well. These individuals would probably be just as concerned about strengthening their test-taking skills as they are about studying for a specific test. Many mental and physical skills are used in preparing for a test. It is important not only to review or study for the examinations, but to make certain that you are alert, relatively free of anxiety, and aware of how to approach standardized tests. Suggestions on developing test-taking skills and preparing psychologically and physically for a test are given. The following section suggests ways of assessing your knowledge of the content of a test and then reviewing and studying the material.

Using This Study Guide

Begin by carefully reading the test description and outline of knowledge and skills required for the examination, if given. As you read through the topics listed there, ask yourself how much you know about each one. Also note the terms, names, and symbols that are mentioned, and ask yourself whether you are familiar with them. This will give you a quick overview of how much you know about the subject. If you are familiar with nearly all the material, you will probably need a minimum of review; however, if less than half of it is familiar, you will probably require substantial study to do well on the test.

If, after reviewing the test description, you find that you need extensive review, delay answering the sample question until you have done some reading in the subject. If you complete them before reviewing the material, you will probably look for the answers as you study, and then they will not be a good assessment of your ability at a later date.

If you think you are familiar with most of the test material, try to answer the sample questions.

Apply the test-taking strategies given. Keeping within the time limit suggested will give you a rough idea of how quickly you should work in order to complete the actual test.

Check your answers against the answer key. If you answered nearly all the questions correctly, you probably do not need to study the subject extensively. If you got about half the questions correct, you ought o review at least one textbook or other suggested materials on the subject. If you answered less than half the questions correctly, you will probably benefit from more extensive reading in the subject and thorough study of one or more textbooks. The textbooks listed are used at many colleges but they are not the only good texts. You will find helpful almost any standard text available to you., such as the textbook used at your college, or earlier editions of texts listed. For some examinations, topic outlines and textbooks may not be available. Take the sample tests in this book and check your answers at the end of each test. Check wrong answers.

Suggestions for Studying

The following suggestions have been gathered from people who have prepared for CLEP examinations or other college-level tests.

1. Define your goals and locate study materials

First, determine your study goals. Set aside a block of time to review the material provided in this book, and then decide which test(s) you will take. Using the suggestions, locate suitable resource materials. If a preparation course is offered by an adult school or college in your area, you might find it helpful to enroll.

2. Find a good place to study

To determine what kind of place you need for studying, ask yourself questions such as: Do I need a quiet place? Does the telephone distract me? Do objects I see in this place remind me of things I should do? Is it too warm? Is it well lit? Am I too comfortable here? Do I have space to spread out my materials? You may find the library more conducive to studying than your home. If you decide to study at home, you might prevent interruptions by other household members by putting a sign on the door of your study room to indicate when you will be available.

3. Schedule time to study

To help you determine where studying best fits into your schedule, try this exercise: Make a list of your daily activities (for example, sleeping, working, and eating) and estimate how many hours per day you spend on each activity. Now, rate all the activities on your list in order of their importance and evaluate your use of time. Often people are astonished at how an average day appears from this perspective. They may discover that they were unaware how large portions of time are spent, or they learn their time can be scheduled in alternative ways. For example, they can remove the least important activities from their day and devote that time to studying or another important activity.

4. Establish a study routine and a set of goals

In order to study effectively, you should establish specific goals and a schedule for accomplishing them. Some people find it helpful to write out a weekly schedule and cross out each study period when it is completed. Others maintain their concentration better by writing down the time when they expect to complete a study task. Most people find short periods of intense study more productive than long stretches of time. For example, they may follow a regular schedule of several 20- or 30-minute study periods with short breaks between them. Some people like to allow themselves rewards as they complete each study goal. It is not essential that you accomplish every goal exactly within your schedule; the point is to be committed to your task.

5. Learn how to take an active role in studying.

If you have not done much studying for some time, you may find it difficult to concentrate at first. Try a method of studying, such as the one outlined below, that will help you concentrate on and remember what you read.

   a. First, read the chapter summary and the introduction. Then you will know what to look for in your reading.

   b. Next, convert the section or paragraph headlines into questions. For example, if you are reading a section entitled, The Causes of the American Revolution, ask yourself: *What were the causes of the American Revolution?* Compose the answer as you read the paragraph. Reading and answering questions aloud will help you understand and remember the material.

c. Take notes on key ideas or concepts as you read. Writing will also help you fix concepts more firmly in your mind. Underlining key ideas or writing notes in your book can be helpful and will be useful for review. Underline only important points. If you underline more than a third of each paragraph, you are probably underlining too much.

d. If there are questions or problems at the end of a chapter, answer or solve them on paper as if you were asked to do them for homework. Mathematics textbooks (and some other books) sometimes include answers to some or all of the exercises. If you have such a book, write your answers before looking at the ones given. When problem-solving is involved, work enough problems to master the required methods and concepts. If you have difficulty with problems, review any sample problems or explanations in the chapter.

e. To retain knowledge, most people have to review the material periodically. If you are preparing for a test over an extended period of time, review key concepts and notes each week or so. Do not wait for weeks to review the material or you will need to relearn much of it.

Psychological and Physical Preparation

Most people feel at least some nervousness before taking a test. Adults who are returning to college may not have taken a test in many years or they may have had little experience with standardized tests. Some younger students, as well, are uncomfortable with testing situations. People who received their education in countries outside the United States may find that many tests given in this country are quite different from the ones they are accustomed to taking.

Not only might candidates find the types of tests and the kinds of questions on them unfamiliar, but other aspects of the testing environment may be strange as well. The physical and mental stress that results from meeting this new experience can hinder a candidate's ability to demonstrate his or her true degree of knowledge in the subject area being tested. For this reason, it is important to go to the test center well prepared, both mentally and physically, for taking the test. You may find the following suggestions helpful.

1. Familiarize yourself, as much as possible, with the test and the test situation before the day of the examination. It will be helpful for you to know ahead of time:

a. How much time will be allowed for the test and whether there are timed subsections.

b. What types of questions and directions appear on the examination.

c. How your test score will be computed.

d. How to properly answer the questions on the computer (See the CLEP Sample on the CLEP website)

  e. In which building and room the examination will be administered. If you don't know where the building is, locate it or get directions ahead of time.

  f. The time of the test administration. You might wish to confirm this information a day or two before the examination and find out what time the building and room will be open so that you can plan to arrive early.

  g. Where to park your car or, if you wish to take public transportation, which bus or train to take and the location of the nearest stop.

  h. Whether smoking will be permitted during the test.

  i. Whether there will be a break between examinations (if you will be taking more than one on the same day), and whether there is a place nearby where you can get something to eat or drink.

2. Go to the test situation relaxed and alert. In order to prepare for the test:

  a. Get a good night's sleep. Last minute cramming, particularly late the night before, is usually counterproductive.

  b. Eat normally. It is usually not wise to skip breakfast or lunch on the day of the test or to eat a big meal just before the test.

  c. Avoid tranquilizers and stimulants. If you follow the other directions in this book, you won't need artificial aids. It's better to be a little tense than to be drowsy, but stimulants such as coffee and cola can make you nervous and interfere with your concentration.

  d. Don't drink a lot of liquids before the test. Having to leave the room during the test will disturb your concentration and take valuable time away from the test.

  e. If you are inclined to be nervous or tense, learn some relaxation exercises and use them before and perhaps during the test.

3. Arrive for the test early and prepared. Be sure to:

  a. Arrive early enough so that you can find a parking place, locate the test center, and get settled comfortably before testing begins. Allow some extra time in case you are delayed unexpectedly.

  b. Take the following with you:

- Your completed Registration/Admission Form
- Two forms of identification – one being a government issued photo ID with signature, such as a driver's license or passport
- Non-mechanical pencil
- A watch so that you can time your progress (digital watches are prohibited)
- Your glasses if you need them for reading or seeing the chalkboard or wall clock

c. Leave all books, papers, and notes outside the test center. You will not be permitted to use your own scratch paper; it will be provided. Also prohibited are calculators, cell phones, beepers, pagers, photo/copy devices, radios, headphones, food, beverages, and several other items.

d. Be prepared for any temperature in the testing room. Wear layers of clothing that can be removed if the room is too hot but will keep you warm if it is too cold.

4. When you enter the test room:

a. Sit in a seat that provides a maximum of comfort and freedom from distraction.

b. Read directions carefully, and listen to all instructions given by the test administrator. If you don't understand the directions, ask for help before test timing begins. If you must ask a question after the test has begun, raise your hand and a proctor will assist you. The proctor can answer certain kinds of questions but cannot help you with the test.

c. Know your rights as a test taker. You can expect to be given the full working time allowed for the test(s) and a reasonably quiet and comfortable place in which to work. If a poor test situation is preventing you from doing your best, ask if the situation can be remedied. If bad test conditions cannot be remedied, ask the person in charge to report the problem in the Irregularity Report that will be sent to ETS with the answer sheets. You may also wish to contact CLEP. Describe the exact circumstances as completely as you can. Be sure to include the test date and name(s) of the test(s) you took. ETS will investigate the problem to make sure it does not happen again, and, if the problem is serious enough, may arrange for you to retake the test without charge.

TAKING THE EXAMINATIONS

A person may know a great deal about the subject being tested, but not do as well as he or she is capable of on the test. Knowing how to approach a test is an important part of the testing process. While a command of test-taking skills cannot substitute for knowledge of the subject matter, it can be a significant factor in successful testing.

Test-taking skills enable a person to use all available information to earn a score that truly reflects his or her ability. There are different strategies for approaching different kinds of test questions. For example, free-response questions require a very different tack than do multiple-choice questions. Other factors, such as how the test will be graded, may also influence your approach to the test and your use of test time. Thus, your preparation for a test should include finding out all you can about the test so that you can use the most effective test-taking strategies.

Before taking a test, you should know approximately how many questions are on the test, how much time you will be allowed, how the test will be scored or graded, what types of questions and directions are on the test, and how you will be required to record your answers.

Taking Multiple-Choice Tests

1. Listen carefully to the instructions given by the test administrator and read carefully all directions before you begin to answer the questions.

2. Note the time that the test administrator starts timing the test. As you proceed, make sure that you are not working too slowly. You should have answered at least half the questions in a section when half the time for that section has passed. If you have not reached that point in the section, speed up your pace on the remaining questions.

3. Before answering a question, read the entire question, including all the answer choices. Don't think that because the first or second answer choice looks good to you, it isn't necessary to read the remaining options. Instructions usually tell you to select the best answer. Sometimes one answer choice is partially correct, but another option is better; therefore, it is usually a good idea to read all the answers before you choose one.

4. Read and consider every question. Questions that look complicated at first glance may not actually be so difficult once you have read them carefully.

5. Do not puzzle too long over any one question. If you don't know the answer after you've considered it briefly, go on to the next question. Make sure you return to the question later.

6. Make sure you record your response properly.

7. In trying to determine the correct answer, you may find it helpful to cross out those options that you know are incorrect, and to make marks next to those you think might be correct. If you decide to skip the question and come back to it later, you will save yourself the time of reconsidering all the options.

8. Watch for the following key words in test questions:

all	generally	never	perhaps
always	however	none	rarely
but	may	not	seldom
except	must	often	sometimes
every	necessary	only	usually

When a question or answer option contains words such as always, every, only, never, and none, there can be no exceptions to the answer you choose. Use of words such as often, rarely, sometimes, and generally indicates that there may be some exceptions to the answer.

9. Do not waste your time looking for clues to right answers based on flaws in question wording or patterns in correct answers. Professionals at the College Board and ETS put

a great deal of effort into developing valid, reliable, fair tests. CLEP test development committees are composed of college faculty who are experts in the subject covered by the test and are appointed by the College Board to write test questions and to scrutinize each question that is included on a CLEP test. Committee members make every effort to ensure that the questions are not ambiguous, that they have only one correct answer, and that they cover college-level topics. These committees do not intentionally include trick questions. If you think a question is flawed, ask the test administrator to report it, or contact CLEP immediately.

Taking Free-Response or Essay Tests

If your college requires the optional free-response or essay portion of a CLEP Composition and Literature exams, you should do some additional preparation for your CLEP test. Taking an essay test is very different from taking a multiple-choice test, so you will need to use some other strategies.

The essay written as part of the English Composition and Essay exam is graded by English professors from a variety of colleges and universities. A process called holistic scoring is used to rate your writing ability.

The optional free-response essays, on the other hand, are graded by the faculty of the college you designate as a score recipient. Guidelines and criteria for grading essays are not specified by the College Board or ETS. You may find it helpful, therefore, to talk with someone at your college to find out what criteria will be used to determine whether you will get credit. If the test requires essay responses, ask how much emphasis will be placed on your writing ability and your ability to organize your thoughts as opposed to your knowledge of subject matter. Find out how much weight will be given to your multiple-choice test score in comparison with your free-response grade in determining whether you will get credit. This will give you an idea where you should expend the greatest effort in preparing for and taking the test.

Here are some strategies you will find useful in taking any essay test:

1. Before you begin to write, read all questions carefully and take a few minutes to jot down some ideas you might include in each answer.

2. If you are given a choice of questions to answer, choose the questions you think you can answer most clearly and knowledgeably.

3. Determine in what order you will answer the questions. Answer those you find the easiest first so that any extra time can be spent on the more difficult questions.

4. When you know which questions you will answer and in what order, determine how much testing time remains and estimate how many minutes you will devote to each question. Unless suggested times are given for the questions or one question appears to require more or less time than the others, allot an equal amount of time to each question.

5. Before answering each question, indicate the number of the question as it is given in the test book. You need not copy the entire question from the question sheet, but it will be helpful to you and to the person grading your test if you indicate briefly the topic you are addressing – particularly if you are not answering the questions in the order in which they appear on the test.

6. Before answering each question, read it again carefully to make sure you are interpreting it correctly. Underline key words, such as those listed below, that often appear in free-response questions. Be sure you know the exact meaning of these words before taking the test.

analyze	demonstrate	enumerate	list
apply	derive	explain	outline
assess	describe	generalize	prove
compare	determine	illustrate	rank
contrast	discuss	interpret	show
define	distinguish	justify	summarize

If a question asks you to outline, define, or summarize, do not write a detailed explanation; if a question asks you to analyze, explain, illustrate, interpret, or show, you must do more than briefly describe the topic.

APPENDIX A 1-12

For a current listing of CLEP Colleges

listing where you can get credit and where you can be tested write:

CLEP, P.O. Box 6600 Princeton, N.J. 08541-6600

Or e-mail: clep @ ets.org or call: 1-609-771-7865

Introductory Macroeconomics

DESCRIPTION OF THE TEST

The Introductory Macroeconomics examination covers material that is usually taught in a one-semester undergraduate course in the principles of macroeconomics. This aspect of economics deals with principles of economics that apply to a total economic system, particularly the general levels of output and income and interrelations among sectors of the economy. The test places particular emphasis on the determinants of aggregate demand and on the monetary and fiscal policies that are appropriate to achieve particular policy objectives. Within this context, candidates are expected to understand concepts such as the multiplier, the accelerator, and balance-of-payments equilibrium; terms such as inflation, deflationary gap, and depreciation; and institutional arrangements such as open-market operations, deficit spending, and flexible exchange rates.

The examination consists of approximately 90 multiple-choice questions to be answered in two separately timed 45-minute sections.

KNOWLEDGE AND SKILLS REQUIRED

The outline below indicates the material covered by the Introductory Macroeconomics examination and the approximate percentage of questions in each category.

Approximate Percent of Examination

Basic concepts of economics applicable to both macroeconomics and microeconomics (20%)

5%	The nature of the economic problem
5%	Production possibilities and alternative costs (opportunity costs)
3%	Comparative advantage; specialization and exchange
2%	The functions of an economic system (what, how, and for whom)
2%	Comparative systems
3%	The role of government in the mixed economy

Macroeconomic concepts (80%)

10%	Measurement of economic performance
	    National income accounting
	    Price index numbers
	    Measurement of unemployment

15%	Money and banking and central banking
10%	Taxation and government expenditure
15%	National income analysis framework

Approximate Percent of Examination	
15%	Business fluctuations and stabilization policies
5%	Economic growth and development
5%	Macroeconomic aspects of international economics
5%	Macroeconomic aspects of income distribution policies

Questions on the test require candidates to demonstrate one or more of the following abilities.

- Understanding of important economic terms and concepts
- Interpretation and manipulation of economic diagrams
- Interpretation and evaluation of economic data
- Application of simple economic models

SAMPLE QUESTIONS

The 25 sample questions given here are similar to questions on the Introductory Macroeconomics examination, but they do not actually appear on the examination.

Before attempting to answer the sample questions, read all the information about the Introductory Macroeconomics examination given above.

Try to answer correctly as many questions as possible within 25 minutes. Then compare your answers with the correct answers that are given on the last page.

Directions: Each of the questions or incomplete statements below is followed by five suggested answers or completions. Select the one that is BEST in each case.

1. Which of the following circumstances would make it impossible for the commercial or private banking system to create money? A(n)
    A. negative discount rate
    B. interest-inelastic demand for investment funds
    C. reserve requirement of 100%
    D. prohibition on Federal Reserve open-market activities
    E. prohibition on bank borrowing from the Federal Reserve

2. The replacement of some portion of the federal personal income tax with a general sales tax would probably result in
    A. greater overall progressivity in the tax structure
    B. lesser overall progressivity in the tax structure
    C. stronger automatic stabilization through the business cycle
    D. increased consumption of liquor, cigarettes, and gasoline
    E. a smaller federal budget deficit

3. A deficit in the United States balance of payments is BEST described as
   A. an excess of commodity imports over commodity exports
   B. an excess of commodity exports over commodity imports
   C. an almost complete depletion of the gold stock
   D. an excess of payments to foreigners over receipts from foreigners
   E. the consequence of an undervalued dollar

Questions 4-6 are based on the five alternatives listed below. In answering each question, assume that the marginal propensity to consume is 4/5.

   A. $10 billion
   B. $20 billion
   C. $30 billion
   D. $40 billion
   E. $50 billion

4. An increase of $10 billion in government expenditures for goods and services would raise the level of national income by how much?

5. A $10 billion increase in the rate of consumer expenditure at each level of the national income would raise the level of national income by how much?

6. A reduction in government tax collections of $10 billion would raise the level of national income by how much?

7. Which of the following reduce(s) the possibility of another depression in the United States as severe as the Great Depression?
   I. The development of deposit insurance
   II. Government willingness to run budgetary deficits in periods of less than full employment
   III. The development of unemployment compensation

   The CORRECT answer is:
   A. I *only*   B. II *only*   C. III *only*
   D. II, III   E. I, II, III

8. Which of the following is net investment as the term is used in economic analysis?
   A. Investment in a share of stock
   B. Investment in savings and loan shares
   C. Construction of an apartment house
   D. Expenditure for a secondhand machine
   E. Purchase of a mortgage

9. If yesterday the rate of exchange between dollars and francs was 1 franc = 20 cents and today it is 1 franc = 25 cents, which of the following must be TRUE?

A. The dollar has appreciated with respect to the franc.
B. The dollar has depreciated with respect to the franc.
C. The dollar has appreciated with respect to gold.
D. The dollar has depreciated with respect to gold.
E. Yesterday the United States balance of payments was in surplus with respect to France.

10. Which of the following means of financing an increase in government spending would be LEAST inflationary?   10.___
    A. Increasing taxes
    B. Printing money
    C. Selling bonds to the Federal Reserve
    D. Selling bonds to commercial banks
    E. Selling bonds to the public (i.e., to individuals and companies)

11. In general, economists agree that the fiscal policy which would do MOST to promote the overall health of the economy is one that   11.___
    A. produces deficits of varying magnitudes at all times
    B. produces surpluses of varying magnitudes at all times
    C. produces deficits during inflations and surpluses during depressions
    D. produces surpluses during inflations and deficits during depressions
    E. is balanced at all times

12. If the Federal Reserve wanted to ease a tight credit situation, it could   12.___
    A. buy bonds in the open market
    B. close commercial banks
    C. call in loans to commercial banks
    D. raise the discount rate
    E. raise reserve requirements

13. Which of the following CORRECTLY describes gross national product?   13.___
    A
    A. theory of the causes of inflation
    B. theory of the causes of unemployment
    C. measure of the total tax receipts of the federal government over a span of time
    D. measure of the total output of an economy over a span of time
    E. measure of the total supply of money in an economy

14. What will be the effect on the economy if the government increases its expenditures and its receipts by an equal amount?   14.___
    A. There will be an expansionary effect on total spending.
    B. There will be no effect on total spending.
    C. There will be a contractionary effect on total spending.
    D. The effect on total spending is unpredictable.
    E. Investment will fall.

15. Which of the following MOST accurately describes the principle of opportunity cost?   15.___
    A. The real cost of using productive resources is the alternative uses that must be sacrificed.
    B. In a free-enterprise system, taking advantage of any economic opportunity involves a money cost.
    C. Because of the law of diminishing returns, increasing national investment in production involves rising costs.
    D. Costs of production vary depending on the different technologies available to firms.
    E. In a free-enterprise system, people often disregard costs of production when the opportunity for profit seems great.

16. Which of the following is used to show the degree of equality or inequality in the distribution of a country's income?   16.___
    The
    A. line of income equality
    B. Lorenz curve
    C. Phillips curve
    D. production-possibility frontier
    E. indifference curve

17.   17.___

    The diagram above indicates which of the following?
    The
    A. public is better off at point B than at point A
    B. public is better off at point A than at point B
    C. total output of the economy is greater at point B than at point A
    D. alternative cost of an additional gun is less at point A than at point B
    E. alternative cost of an additional gun is higher at point A than at point B

18. If the Federal Reserve wishes to expand the money supply, it is MOST likely to succeed by   18.___
    A. selling bonds to the public and spending the revenues
    B. selling bonds to the public and not spending the revenues
    C. increasing the discount rate charged to member banks

D. buying bonds from the public and increasing commercial-bank reserve requirements
E. buying bonds from the public and reducing commercial-bank reserve requirements

19. All of the following are methods of curbing inflation EXCEPT
    A. increasing the supply of consumer goods
    B. increasing income tax rates
    C. increasing the supply of money
    D. increasing interest rates
    E. restricting installment buying

20. In an economy operating at full capacity (or full employment), an increase in government purchases must result in a(n)
    A. decrease in real consumption, real private investment, and/or real net exports
    B. decrease in real gross national product
    C. increase in real gross national product
    D. increase in the rate of inflation
    E. increase in the unemployment rate

21. Which of the following are characteristic of pure socialism?
    I. All capital goods and natural resources are owned by the government.
    II. Decisions as to what goods are to be produced and how they are to be produced are made by government officials.
    III. Individuals are free to produce any good or service that they wish to produce.
    IV. All human wants are satisfied.
    V. All capital goods and natural resources are owned by individuals, and their ownership is distributed equally among individuals.

    The CORRECT answer is:
    A. I, II   B. I, III   C. III, IV
    D. III, V   E. IV, V

22. If the federal government of the United States is running a fiscal deficit, which of the following must be TRUE? The
    A. United States is importing more goods and services than it is exporting
    B. money supply of the United States is rising
    C. unemployment rate of the United States is falling
    D. debt of the federal government of the United States is rising
    E. rate of inflation in the United States is rising

23. If the marginal propensity to consume is 1/3, the multiplier will be
    A. 0.33   B. 1.33   C. 1.50   D. 1.67   E. 2.00

24. If an individual borrows $1,000 from a bank and the loan is credited to the individual's deposit account, which of the following is CORRECT?
The
- A. money supply is increased by $1,000
- B. bank has loaned the individual what someone else has deposited
- C. bank has loaned the individual $1,000 of its resources
- D. bank's assets are decreased by $1,000
- E. bank is engaging in open-market operations

25.

	Shoes	Suits
Country A	5 labor-hours	10 labor-hours
Country B	10 labor-hours	30 labor-hours

The table above indicates labor-hours needed to produce a single unit of each of two commodities in each of two countries. (Labor is the only factor used to produce the two commodities.)
Which of the following statements is CORRECT?
- I. Country B has an absolute disadvantage in both commodities but a comparative advantage in the production of shoes.
- II. Country B has an absolute disadvantage in both commodities but a comparative advantage in the production of suits.
- III. Mutually advantageous trade between the two countries can occur when the international exchange rate equals 2.5 pairs of shoes for 1 suit.

The CORRECT answer is:
- A. I *only*
- B. II *only*
- C. III *only*
- D. I, III
- E. II, III

OPTIONAL FREE-RESPONSE SECTION

If your college requires that the optional free-response section be taken in addition to the multiple-choice examination, you should review the following information.

The optional free-response section of the Introductory Macroeconomics examination calls for much the same knowledge as does the multiple-choice test. It requires candidates to select and organize materials related to macroeconomic issues, and to present them logically and accurately. Candidates are asked to answer three of four questions offered within a 90-minute period.

STUDY RESOURCES

There are many introductory economics textbooks that vary greatly in difficulty. The following books are among the more widely used for introductory courses in the principles of economics. All the books are published in one-volume editions, which cover both microeconomics and macroeconomics. Except for the textbook by McConnell, all of them are also published in two-volume editions, with one volume covering macroeconomics and the other microeconomics. All the references cover the topics in the content outlines of the Introductory Macroeconomics and Introductory Microeconomics examinations.

To broaden your knowledge of economic issues, you may read relevant articles published in the economics periodicals that are available in most college libraries; for example, CHALLENGE magazine contains articles by and interviews of major economists and analyses of current economic controversies with emphasis on public policy. The WALL STREET JOURNAL may also enhance your understanding of economic issues.

Textbooks

Baumol, William J. and Alan S. Blinder, ECONOMICS, PRINCIPLES AND POLICY, 4th ed. New York: Harcourt Brace Jovanovich, Inc., 1988.

Lipsey, Richard C., Peter O. Steiner and Douglas D. Purvis, ECONOMICS, 9th ed. New York: Harper and Row Pubs., Inc., 1990.

Mansfield, Edwin, ECONOMICS: PRINCIPLES, PROBLEMS, DECISIONS, 6th ed. New York: W.W. Norton Co., Inc., 1989.

McConnell, Campbell R., ECONOMICS: PRINCIPLES, PROBLEMS AND POLICIES, 10th ed. New York: McGraw-Hill Book Co., 1987.

Miller, Roger LeRoy, ECONOMICS TODAY, 6th ed. New York: Harper and Row, Publishers, 1988.

Samuelson, Paul A. and William D. Nordhaus, ECONOMICS, 13th ed. New York: McGraw-Hill Book Co., 1989.

KEY (CORRECT ANSWERS)

1. C
2. B
3. D
4. E
5. E

6. D
7. E
8. C
9. B
10. A

11. D
12. A
13. D
14. A
15. A

16. B
17. E
18. E
19. C
20. A

21. A
22. D
23. C
24. A
25. D

HOW TO TAKE A TEST

You have studied hard, long, and conscientiously.

With your official admission card in hand, and your heart pounding, you have been admitted to the examination room.

You note that there are several hundred other applicants in the examination room waiting to take the same test.

They all appear to be equally well prepared.

You know that nothing but your best effort will suffice. The "moment of truth" is at hand: you now have to demonstrate objectively, in writing, your knowledge of content and your understanding of subject matter.

You are fighting the most important battle of your life—to pass and/or score high on an examination which will determine your career and provide the economic basis for your livelihood.

What extra, special things should you know and should you do in taking the examination?

BEFORE THE TEST

YOUR PHYSICAL CONDITION IS IMPORTANT

If you are not well, you can't do your best work on tests. If you are half asleep, you can't do your best either. Here are some tips:

1. Get about the same amount of sleep you usually get. Don't stay up all night before the test, either partying or worrying—DON'T DO IT.

2. If you wear glasses, be sure to wear them when you go to take the test. This goes for hearing aids, too.

3. If you have any physical problems that may keep you from doing your best, be sure to tell the person giving the test. If you are sick or in poor health, you really cannot do your best on any test. You can always come back and take the test some other time.

AT THE TEST

EXAMINATION TECHNIQUES

1. Read the *general* instructions carefully. These are usually printed on the first page of the examination booklet. As a rule, these instructions refer to the timing of the examination; the fact that you should not start work until the signal and must stop work at a signal, etc. If there are any *special* instructions, such as a choice of questions to be answered, make sure that you note this instruction carefully.

2. **When you are ready to start work on the examination**, that is as soon as the signal has been given, read the instructions to each question booklet, underline any key words or phrases, such as *least, best, outline, describe,* and the like. In this way you will tend to answer as requested rather than discover on reviewing your paper that you *listed without describing,* that you selected the *worst* choice rather than the *best* choice, etc.

3. If the examination is of the objective or so-called multiple-choice type, that is, each question will also give a series of possible answers: A, B, C, or D, and you are called upon to select the best answer and write the letter next to that answer on your answer paper, it is advisable to start answering each question in turn. There may be anywhere from 50 to 100 such questions in the three or four hours allotted and you can see how much time would be taken if you read through all the questions before beginning to answer any. Furthermore, if you come across a question or a group of questions which you know would be difficult to answer, it would undoubtedly affect your handling of all the other questions.

4. If the examination is of the essay-type and contains but a few questions, it is a moot point as to whether you should read all the questions before starting to answer any one. Of course if you are given a choice, say five out of seven and the like, then it is essential to read all the questions so you can eliminate the two which are most difficult. If, however, you are asked to answer all the questions, there may be danger in trying to answer the easiest one first because you may find that you will spend too much time on it. The best technique is to answer the first question, then proceed to the second, etc.

5. Time your answers. Before the examination begins, write down the time it started, then add the time allowed for the examination and write down the time it must be completed, then divide the time available somewhat as follows:

    a. If 3½ hours are allowed, that would be 210 minutes. If you have 80 objective-type questions, that would be an average of about 2½ minutes per question. Allow yourself no more than 2 minutes per question, or a total of 160 minutes, which will permit about 50 minutes to review.

    b. If for the time allotment of 210 minutes, there are 7 essay questions to answer, that would average about 30 minutes a question. Give yourself only 25 minutes per question so that you have about 35 minutes to review.

6. The most important instruction is *to read each question* and make sure you know what is wanted. The second most important instruction is to *time yourself properly* so that you answer every question. The third most important instruction is to *answer every question*. Guess if you have to but include something for each question, Remember that you will receive no credit for a blank and will probably receive some credit if you write something in answer to an essay question. If you guess a letter, say "B" for a multiple-choice question, you may have guessed right. If you leave a blank as the answer to a multiple-choice question, the examiners may respect your feelings but it will not add a point to your score. Some exams may penalize you for wrong answers, so in such cases *only*, you may not want to guess unless you have some basis for your answer.

7. Suggestions

    a. Objective-Type Questions

    (1) Examine the question booklet for proper sequence of pages and questions.

    (2) Read all instructions carefully.

    (3) Skip any question which seems too difficult; return to it after all other questions have been answered.

    (4) Apportion your time properly; do not spend too much time on any single question or group of questions.

    (5) Note and underline key words—*all, most, fewest, least, best, worst, same, opposite*.

    (6) Pay particular attention to negatives.

    (7) Note unusual option, e.g., unduly long, short, complex, different or similar in content to the body of the question.

    (8) Observe the use of "hedging" words—*probably, may, most likely, etc.*

    (9) Make sure that your answer is put next to the same number as the question.

    (10) Do not second guess unless you have good reason to believe the second answer is definitely more correct.

    (11) Cross out original answer if you decide another answer is more accurate; do not erase, *until* you are ready to hand your paper in.

    (12) Answer all questions; guess unless instructed otherwise.

    (13) Leave time for review.

b. Essay-Type Questions
   - (1) Read each question carefully.
   - (2) Determine exactly what is wanted. Underline key words or phrases.
   - (3) Decide on outline or paragraph answer.
   - (4) Include many different points and elements unless asked to develop any one or two points or elements.
   - (5) Show impartiality by giving pros and cons unless directed to select one side only.
   - (6) Make and write down any assumptions you find necessary to answer the question.
   - (7) Watch your English, grammar, punctuation, choice of words.
   - (8) Time your answers; don't crowd material.

8. Answering the Essay Question

   Most essay questions can be answered by framing the specific response around several key words or ideas. Here are a few such key words or ideas:

   M's: manpower, materials, methods, money, management

   P's: purpose, program, policy, plan, procedure, practice, problems, pitfalls, personnel, public relations

   a. Six basic steps in handling problems:
      - (1) preliminary plan and background development
      - (2) collect information, data and facts
      - (3) analyze and interpret information, data and facts
      - (4) analyze and develop solutions as well as make recommendations
      - (5) prepare report and sell recommendations
      - (6) install recommendations and follow up effectiveness

   b. Pitfalls to Avoid
      - (1) *Taking Things for Granted*
        A statement of the situation does not necessarily imply that each of the elements is necessarily true; for example, a complaint may be invalid and biased so that all that can be taken for granted is that a complaint has been registered
      - (2) *Considering only one side of a situation*
        Wherever possible, indicate several alternatives and then point out the reasons you selected the best one.
      - (3) *Failing to indicate follow up*
        Whenever your answer indicates action on your part, make certain that you will take proper follow-up action to see how successful your recommendations, procedures, or actions turn out to be.
      - (4) *Taking too long in answering any single question*
        Remember to time your answers properly.

EXAMINATION SECTION

EXAMINATION SECTION
TEST 1

DIRECTIONS: Each question or incomplete statement is followed by several suggested answers or completions. Select the one that BEST answers the question or completes the statement. *PRINT THE LETTER OF THE CORRECT ANSWER IN THE SPACE AT THE RIGHT.*

1. Which of the following implies the law of diminishing returns?

    a. As all inputs are doubled, output less than doubles.
    b. As one input is increased, additions to output get smaller.
    c. As all inputs are doubled, output more than doubles.
    d. As one input is increased, output less than doubles.

2. Which of the following will NOT cause the economy's production possibility frontier to shift out?

    a. The discovery of previously unknown oil fields.
    b. An improvement in technology.
    c. An increase in the stock of capital.
    d. A decrease in the unemployment rate.

3. In a two-good economy, if the opportunity cost of producing a good DECREASES as more of that good is produced, the economy's production possibility frontier will be

    a. "Bowed inward" toward the origin.
    b. "Bowed outward" from the origin.
    c. A straight line.
    d. Impossible to say whether a straight line or a bowed line.

4. Fantasia is occupied by two tribes: Nates and Bens. Nates live in Nateland and Bens live in Benland, which are two geographically separate regions. Fantasia only grows wheat and soybeans. Wheat can only grow in Nateland and soybeans can only grow in Benland. Different tribes can work on each other's land. The following annual combinations constitute Fantasia's production possibilities frontier (PPF).

Possibility	Wheat (in tons)	Soybeans (in tons)
A	0	14
B	2	12
C	4	9
D	6	5
E	8	0

a. Draw Fantasia's PPF by plotting the points A, B, C, D, E and joining the dots (with wheat on the horizontal axis).

b. The World Bank supplies Fantasia with a crop duster plane and a new insect spray that kills the insects that only prey on wheat (and does nothing to the insects that prey on soybeans). Once wheat crops are sprayed, the output of wheat will double. Draw the new PPF of Fantasia once the crop duster plane is in use.

c. Now, thanks to new chemical additives, Fantasia gets a more effective spray that kills insects affecting both crops (so that the soybean yield could double, too, if sprayed).

  1. Even though Fantasia now has new chemicals, the country has only one plane and thus can either spray Nateland or Benland, but not both. Draw the new PPF of Fantasia if only Nateland or Benland can be sprayed.

  2. A huge swarm of insects is now approaching Fantasia. Unless sprayed with the new spray, these insects will eat the entire crop in Nateland and Benland. Recalling that Fantasia still has only one plane (and can only spray Nateland or Benland but not both), draw the new PPF of Fantasia once the insect threat is realized.

d. Go back to the PPF in part (a). The people of Fantasia, Nates and Bens, now embrace a new religion that strictly prohibits the consumption of soybeans. Explain how the PPF in part (a) will change.

KEY (CORRECT ANSWERS)

1. (1 point) The answer is (b). Other choices are fiddling around the concept of returns to scale.

2. (1 point) The answer is (d). The PPF (production possibilities frontier) is a theoretical construct that demonstrates the limits of production possibilities in an ideal world, i.e., full and efficient use of all resources. Unemployment indicates less than full use of resources and hence corresponds to a point inside the PPF. Reducing unemployment moves the economy towards the PPF but does not shift it.

3. (2 points) The answer is (a).

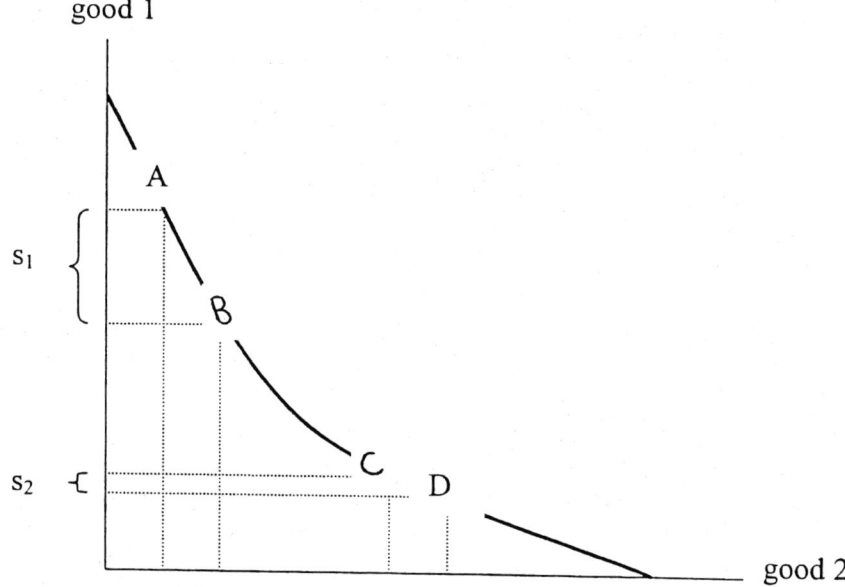

Examine the figure above. Starting from point A, if we want to produce more of good 2 (move from point A to B) we have to give up s_1 amount of good 1. However, at a point where more of good 2 is produced (point C), to have the same increase in good 2 that we had by moving from A to B (thus now moving from C to D), we sacrifice a smaller amount of good 1, only of the amount s_1.

4.a. (1 point)

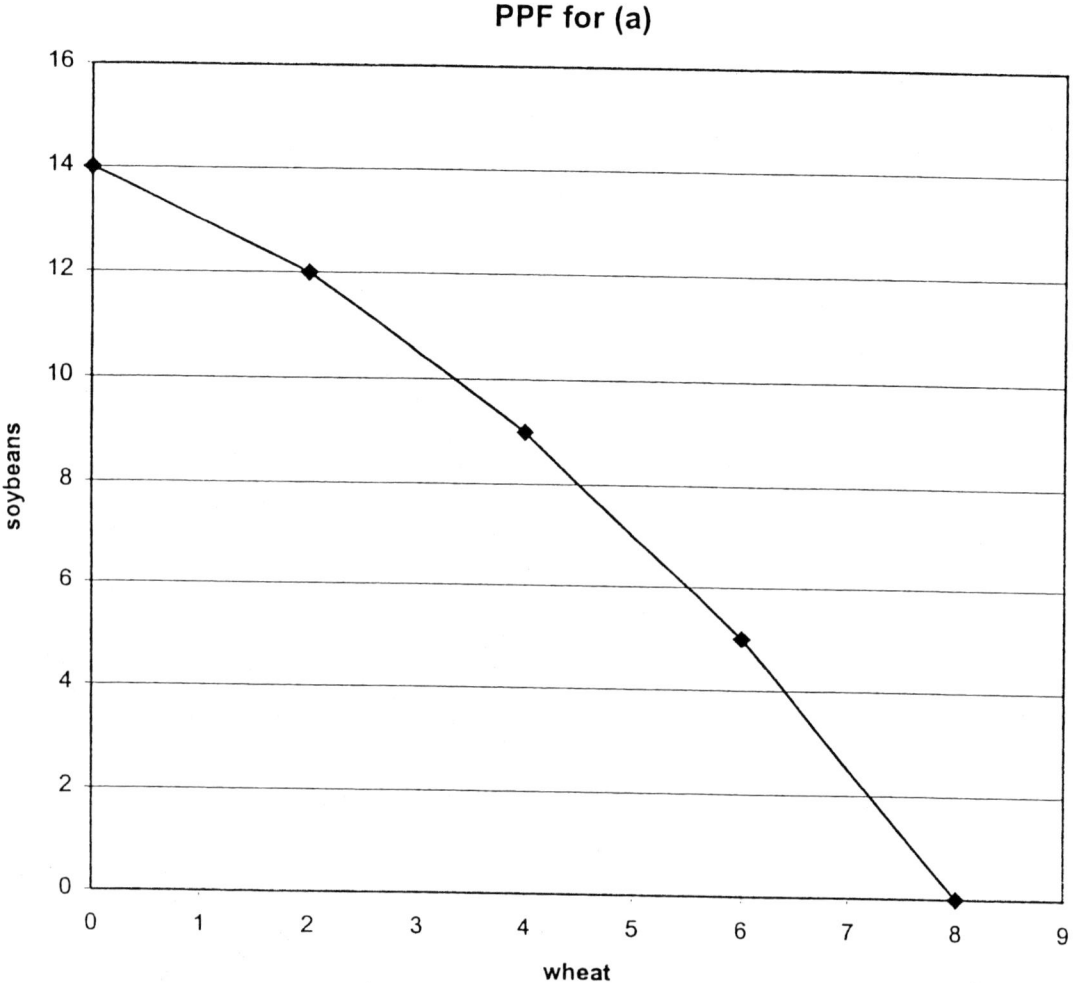

4.b. (1 point)

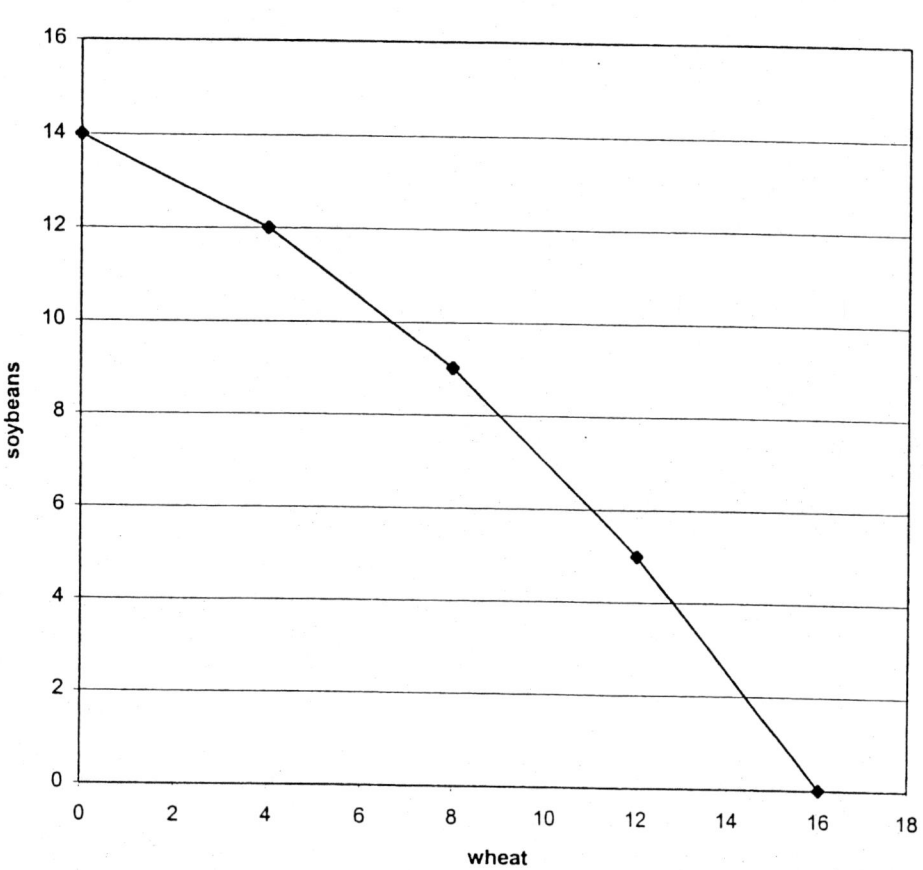

4.c.1. (2 points)

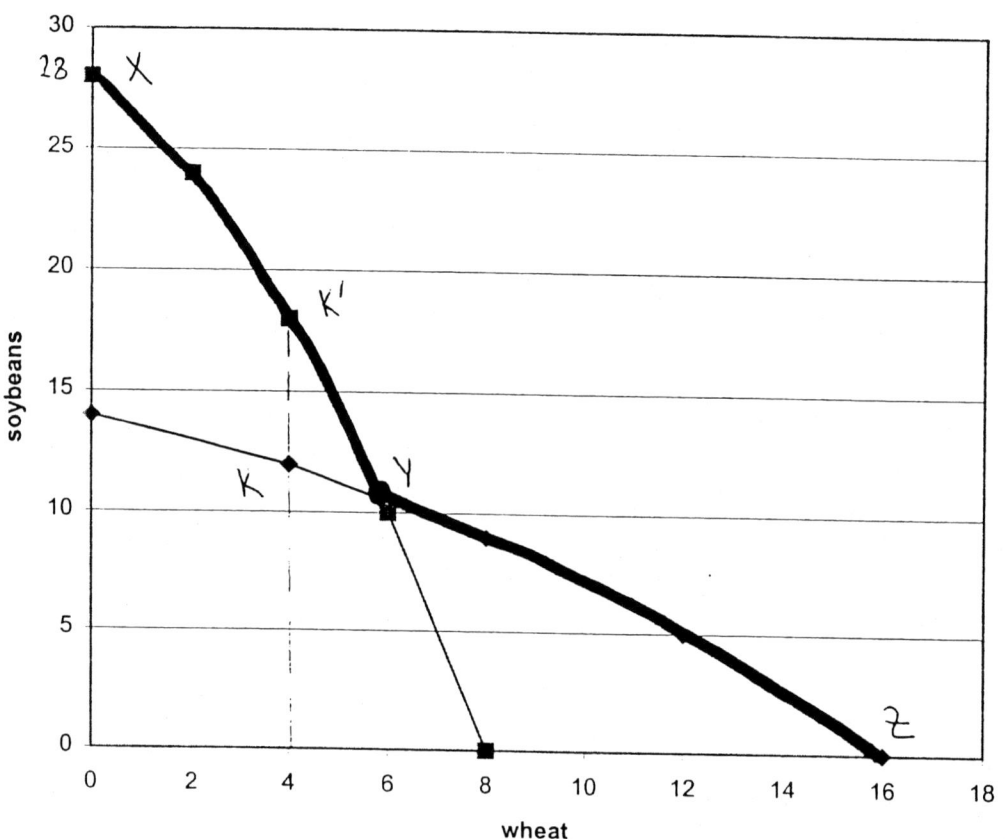

PPF for 4.c.1.

The new PPF is the outer envelope of the two PPFs, shown by the heavy line connecting the points X, Y and Z. That is because the plane can spray Nateland or Benland, so we have two possibilities. In the first case, the wheat yield doubles but the soybean yield remains the same and in the second case, vice versa. Since we are looking for the frontier, we are interested in those points where we get the best possible yield of wheat and soybeans. That is why we do not include the parts of the two intersecting PPFs that lie within the heavy-lined PPF (XYZ): we can always do better than those points. For example, take the point K. The point K' gives the same amount of wheat as point K but more of soybeans. So, our "best" cannot be K, since K' does better. If you try it yourself you will see that we cannot do this with any point on XYZ. Along XYZ, if we want to increase the production of any crop, we *have to* reduce the production of the other.

4.c.2. (1 point)

PPF for 4.c.2.

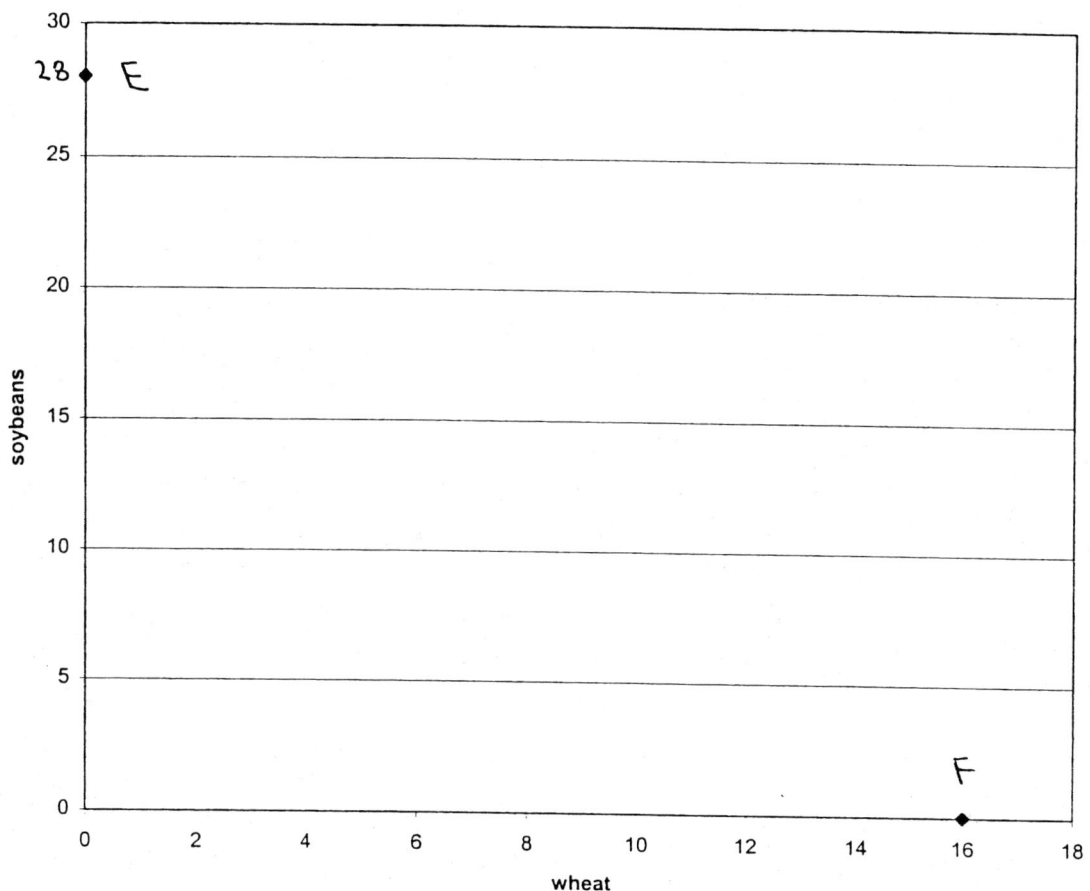

Now, if Nateland is sprayed we get 16 tons of wheat (doubled yield) but the insects eat all of the soybeans. If Benland is sprayed, we get 28 tons of soybeans (doubled yield) but the insects eat all the wheat. So the PPF collapses to 2 points, namely E and F.

4.d. (1 point) Nothing changes. What is happening on the demand side does not alter the PPF in any way. Even if no one is consuming soybeans, Fantasia is still *capable* of producing just the same combinations of wheat and soybeans.

TEST 2

DIRECTIONS: Each question or incomplete statement is followed by several suggested answers or completions. Select the one that BEST answers the question or completes the statement. *PRINT THE LETTER OF THE CORRECT ANSWER IN THE SPACE AT THE RIGHT.*

1. Which of the following will *necessarily* occur when there is a simultaneous increase in demand and a decrease in supply (that is, the demand curve shifts right and the supply curve shifts left)?

    (a) an increase in equilibrium price.
    (b) a decrease in equilibrium price.
    (c) an increase in equilibrium quantity.
    (d) a decrease in equilibrium quantity.

2. **Refer to Figure 4.6.** The number of pizzas this restaurant sells per week increases from 500 to 700. This could be caused by

    (a) an improvement in technology that reduces the cost of making pizza.
    (b) a decrease in the price of one of the ingredients used to make pizza.
    (c) an increase in the price of pizza.
    (d) a decrease in the demand for pizza.

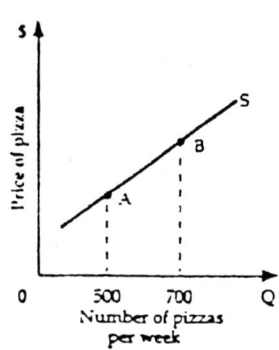

Figure 4.6

3. **Refer to Figure 4.9.** In the rollerblade market, you accurately predict that

    (a) price will increase, the quantity demanded will fall, and the quantity supplied will rise.
    (b) price will increase, the quantity demanded will rise, and the quantity supplied will fall.
    (c) price will decrease, the quantity demanded will fall, and the quantity supplied will fall.
    (d) price will decrease, the quantity demanded will rise, and the quantity supplied will fall.

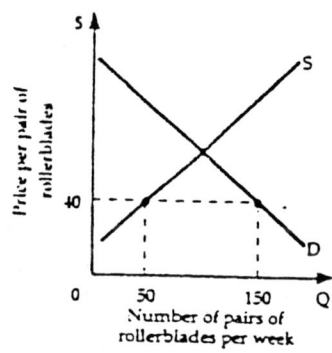

Figure 4.9

4. Suppose there are only two companies supplying "on-line services" (that is, access to the Internet) for a small island economy in the Pacific. They are willing to provide the following amounts of on-line time at various prices:

Amarillo Online		Compus Werve	
Price ($/Hour)	Time Provided (Millions of Hours per week)	Price ($/Hour)	Time Provided (Millions of Hours per week)
1	5	1	5
2	12	2	8
3	16	3	14
4	22	4	18
5	27	5	23

(a) Draw the aggregate supply curve for on-line services for this economy.

(b) According to a reputable marketing research firm, the aggregate demand for the on-line services in the economy is indicated by the following table:

AGGREGATE DEMAND

Price ($/Hour)	Time Provided (Millions of Hours per week)
1	40
2	35
3	30
4	25
5	20

Draw and label the aggregate demand curve on the same diagram you drew in answer to (a). What is the equilibrium price and quantity?

(c) Suppose the Government imposes a price ceiling of $4 per hour on on-line services (i.e., nobody can sell on-line services above $4). Indicate the impact of this policy on the price and quantity of on-line services, using a supply-and-demand diagram.

(d) On-line services and computers are complements. One of the two on-line service companies is destroyed by fire, raising the price of on-line services. This rise in the price of on-line services, claims an economist, will shift the supply curve for computers, because at lower computer prices, computer suppliers will supply less. Justify, qualify, or repudiate that claim. (Use a supply-and-demand diagram to illustrate your main points.)

KEY (CORRECT ANSWERS)

1. (1 point) a.

2. (1 point) c.

3. (1 point) a.

4. (a) (2 points) Aggregate supply is found by horizontally adding up the supply curves of Amarillo Online and Compus Were.

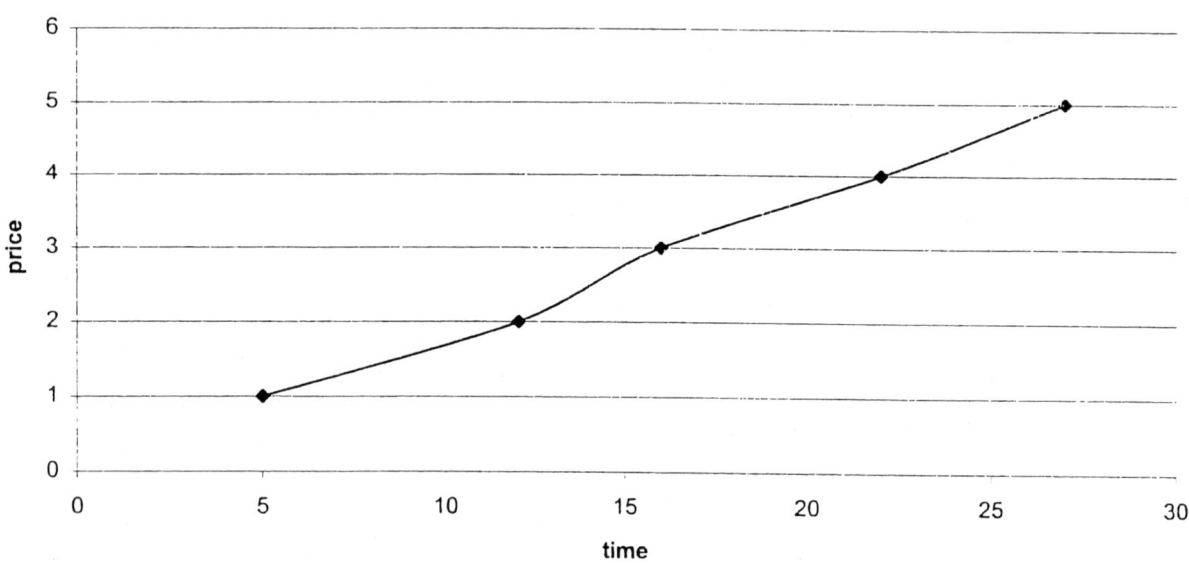

Compus Werve

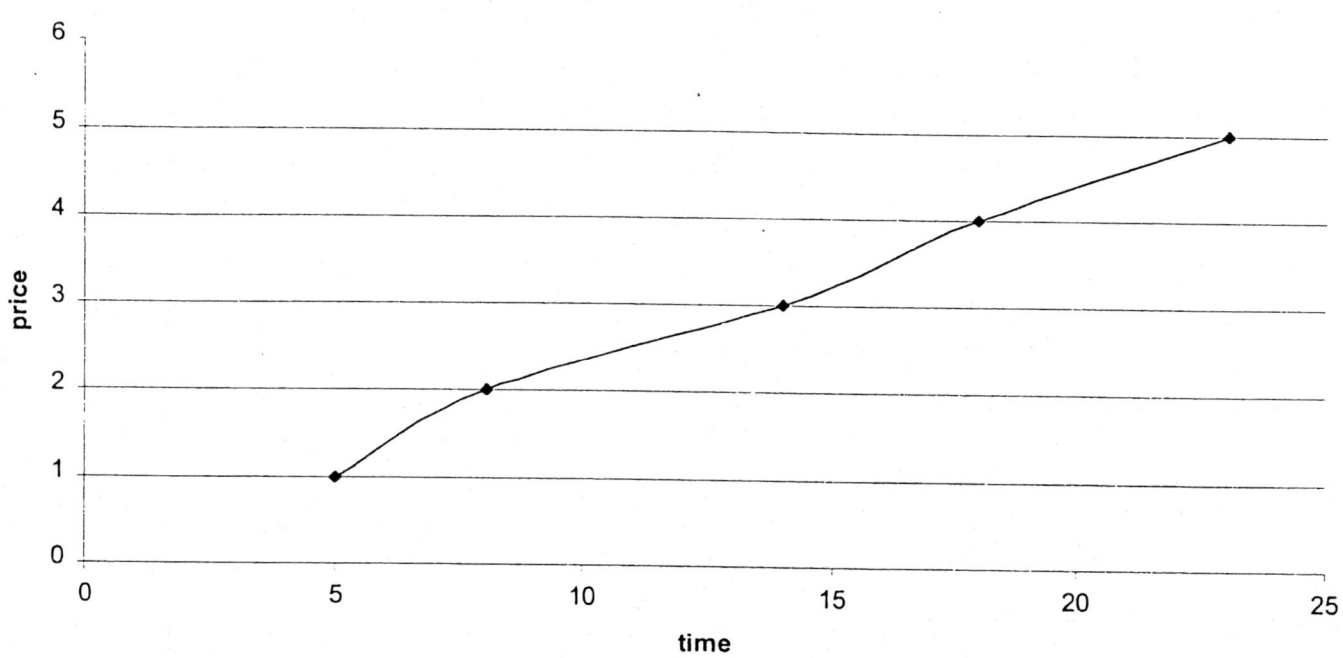

Aggregate Supply

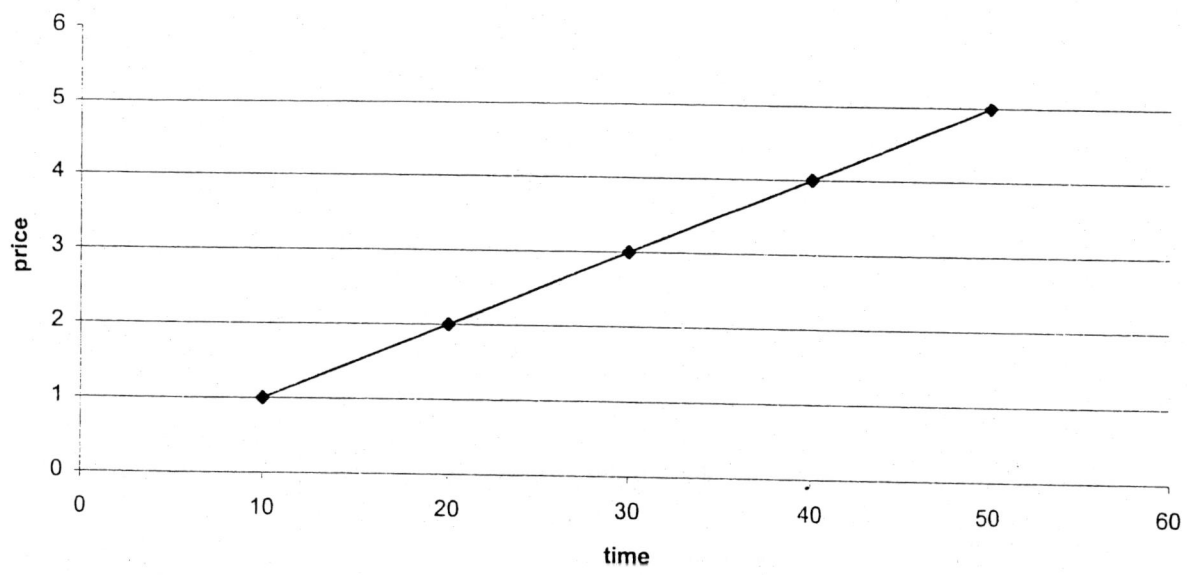

(b) (1 point) The equilibrium price and quantity are determined by the intersection of the aggregate demand and supply curves. The equilibrium price is 3 and the equilibrium quantity is 30.

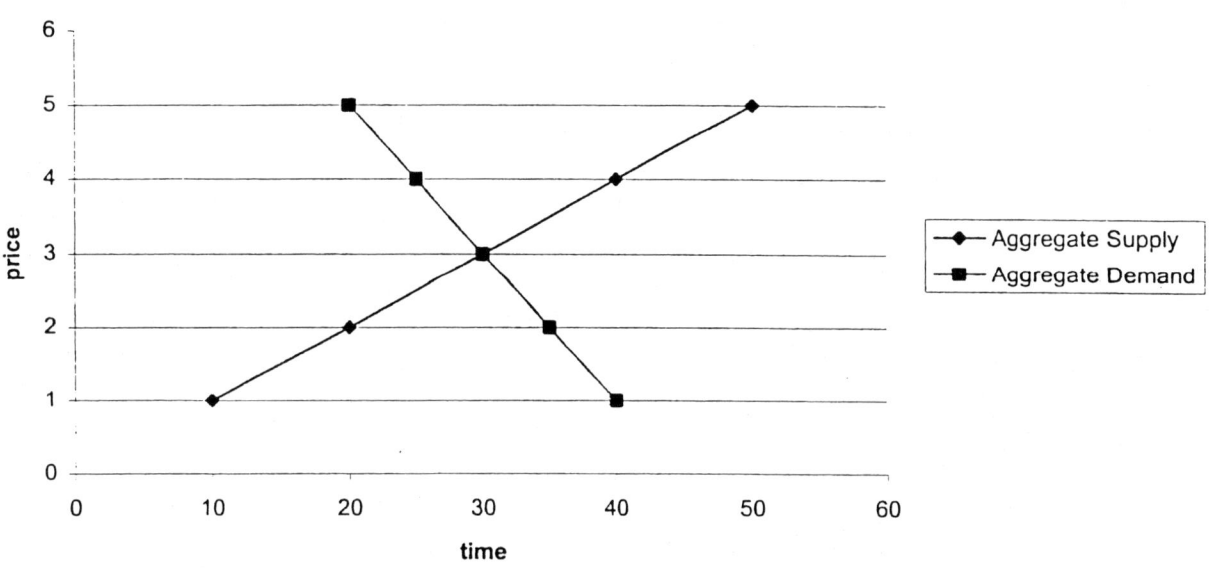

(c) (2 points) Nothing changes. Since the equilibrium price is already below the price ceiling, the existing equilibrium is still available. The market will clear at the same equilibrium.

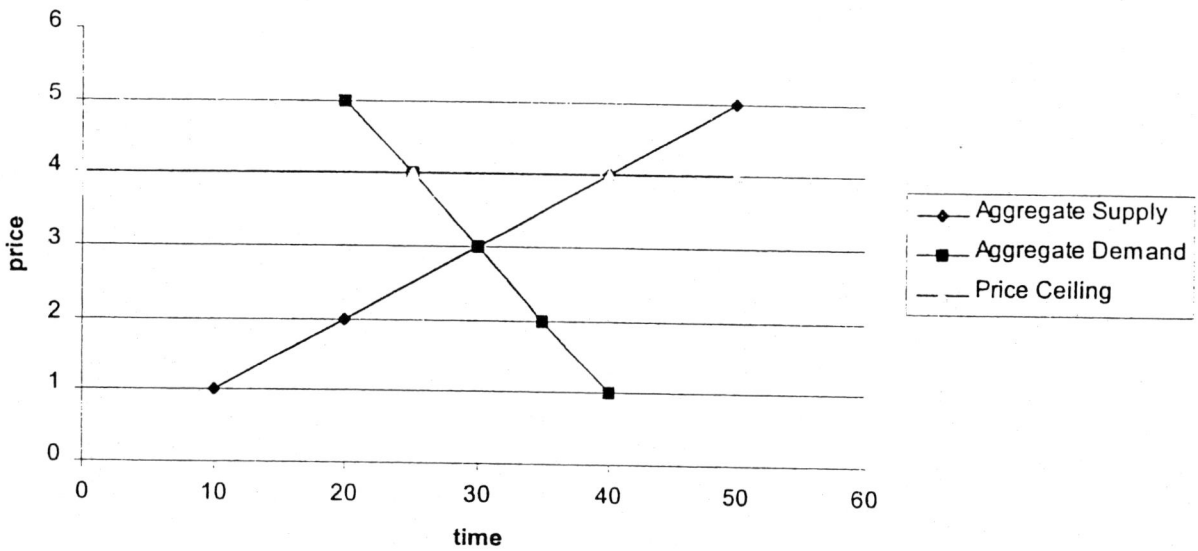

(d) (2 points) The rise in the price of on-line services will shift the demand curve to the left because on-line services are complementary to computers. Hence, now people will demand fewer computers at any price. This will not affect the supply curve for computers but the at the new equilibrium (Point B) equilibrium price and quantity will be lower than those at the old equilibrium (Point A).

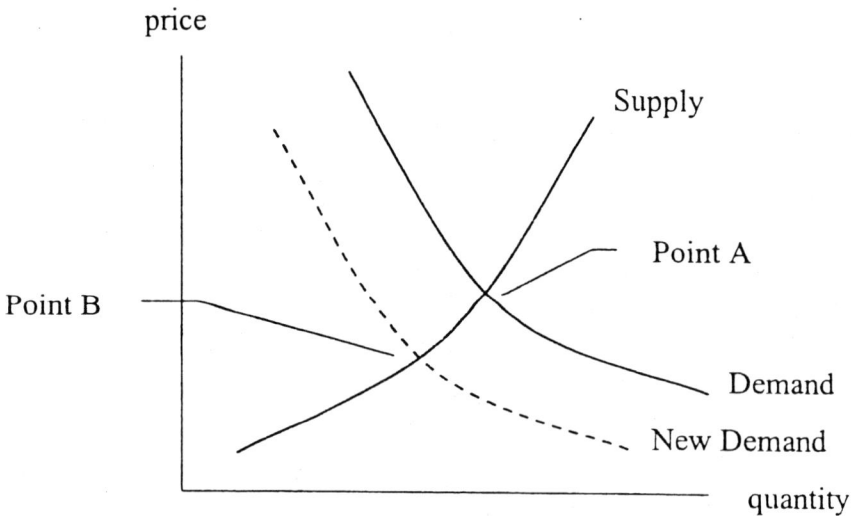

TEST 3

DIRECTIONS: Each question or incomplete statement is followed by several suggested answers or completions. Select the one that BEST answers the question or completes the statement. *PRINT THE LETTER OF THE CORRECT ANSWER IN THE SPACE AT THE RIGHT.*

1. Which of the following transactions would be counted in GDP?

    a   The wood you purchase to build yourself bookshelves in your room.
    b   An economics textbook you purchase with the intent of selling it after your course is over.
    c   Rent paid by Japanese tenants to an American who owns apartments in Tokyo.
    d   The profit-sharing check that an employee receives this year.
    e   The bicycles that a store adds to its inventory this year but is unable to sell.
    f   Interest paid on consumer loans by households.
    g   The commissions earned by a real estate agent in selling houses.

2. Which of the following would NOT be counted as investment in the national income accounts?

    a   Building of a factory by General Motors.
    b   Increase in General Motors inventories of raw materials.
    c   Installation of a new assembly line at General Motors.
    d   Purchase of a share of stock in General Motors by an employee of General Motors.

3. Which of the following is NOT included in 1998's GDP?

    a   The value of a car produced in the United States and exported to England.
    b   The profit earned in 1998 from selling a stock that you purchased in 1990.
    c   The value of a computer chip that is used in the production of a personal computer.
    d   The commission earned by an employment counselor when she locates a job for a client.

Consider a simple economy consisting of consumers, farmers, a grocery store and a restaurant. Assume the following transactions take place within a year.

1. Farmers sell $3,000 worth of potatoes to the grocery store, and $2,500 worth of potatoes to the restaurant.

2. Fishermen sell $5,000 worth of fish to the grocery store, and $3,500 worth of fish to the restaurant.

3. The grocery store, after cleaning and wrapping, sells potatoes (now worth $3,500) and fish (now worth $6,000, to consumers.

4. The restaurant serves "fish and chips" (worth $10,000) to their customers.

   (a) What is the value of intermediate goods used by the

   1. Farmers
   2. Fishermen
   3. Grocery store
   4. Restaurant.

   (b) What is the total "value added" in the economy?
   (c) What are the total sales of final goods in the economy? (Give a dollar value.)
   (d) What, if any, is the relationship between "valued added" and "total sales of final goods" in the economy? (Answer in one sentence.)
   (e) A foreign firm now buys the restaurant. Under the new owners, the restaurant still uses the same amount of intermediate goods and sells the same amount of "fish and chips." But the new foreign owners realize that the previous owners had forgotten to charge $1000 each year for the wearing out (or the depreciation) of the restaurant's cooking equipment. Explain how each of these changes ((i) new foreign ownership and (ii) restaurant depreciation charges) affect the value of GDP (gross domestic product). Use one sentence only for each explanation.

KEY (CORRECT ANSWERS)

Multiple Choice

1. (1.5 points) (a), (b), (d), (e), (f) and (g) are counted in GDP but (c) is not counted in GDP (Case & Fair are ambiguous about (f), so we accepted both answers).

2. (0.5 point) The answer is (d).

3. (0.5 point) The answer is (b).

Long Answer Questions

(a) (2 points)

1. The value of intermediate goods used by the farmers is zero.

2. The value of intermediate goods used by the fishermen is zero.

3. The value of intermediate goods used by the grocery store is $3,000 + $5,000 = $8,000.

4. The value of intermediate goods used by the restaurant is $2,500 + $3,500 = $6,000.

(b) (2 points).

The value added by the farmers is ($3,000 + $2,500) – 0 = $5,500.

The value added by the fishermen is ($5,000 + $3,500) – 0 = $8,500.

The value added by the grocery is ($3,500 + $6,000) - ($3,000 + $5,000) = $1,500.

The value added by the restaurant is $10,000 - ($2,500 + $3,500) = $4,000.

Therefore the total value added in the economy is $5,500 + $8,500 + $1,500 + $4,000 = $19,500.

(c) (1 point)

Sales of final goods by the farmers = 0

Sales of final goods by the fishermen = 0

Sales of final goods by the grocery = $9,500.

Sales of final goods by the restaurant = $10,000

Therefore the total sales of final goods in the economy is 0 + 0 + $9,500 + $10,000 = $19,500.

(d) (0.5 point) "Value added" and the "total sales of final goods" in the economy are exactly equal.

(e) (i) (0.5 point) New foreign ownership does not affect the value of GDP.

(ii) (1 point) Restaurant depreciation charges do not affect the value of GDP.

TEST 4

DIRECTIONS: Each question or incomplete statement is followed by several suggested answers or completions. Select the one that BEST answers the question or completes the statement. *PRINT THE LETTER OF THE CORRECT ANSWER IN THE SPACE AT THE RIGHT.*

The General Accounting Office sends you the following US economic data for 1997. (All figures are in billions of dollars).

A	Payment of Factor Income to Rest of the World	128.4
B	Receipt of Factor Income from Rest of the World	121.6
C	Subsidies	40.1
D	Proprietors' Income	438
E	Personal Taxes	705.7
F	Rental Income	7.3
G	Capital Consumption Allowance (Depreciation)	610.5
H	Personal Consumption Expenditure on Services	2083.4
I	Total Expenditure on Durable Goods	1252
J	Total Expenditure on Non-Durable Goods	507.1
K	Indirect Taxes	522.4
L	Government Spending	1076.2
M	Exports	748.3
N	Transfer Payments	733.4
O	Imports	705.9
P	Dividends	40.8
Q	Social Insurance Payments	511.1
R	Corporate Profits	321.5
S	Personal Interest Income	221.3
T	Net Interest Income	487.6
U	Personal Consumption Expenditure	3842.5
V	Compensation of Employees	3404.5

1. Calculate Gross Domestic Product (GDP), Gross National Product (GNP), and Net National Product (NNP).

2. Calculate Gross Investment and Net Investment.

3. Calculate Personal Income and Disposable Income.

KEY (CORRECT ANSWERS)

1. A. Calculate GDP *(1 point)*
   Using the income approach (table 7.3 from Case & Fair), we have

   GDP = National Income + Depreciation + Indirect taxes minus subsidies + Net factor payments to the rest of the world

   = [Compensation of employees + Proprietors' income + Corporate profits + Net interest + Rental income] + Depreciation + Indirect taxes minus subsidies + Net factor payments to the rest of the world

   = [3404.5 + 438 + 321.5 + 487.6 + 7.3] + 610.5 + (522.4 − 40.1) + (128.4 − 121.6)

   = **5758.5**.

   B. Calculate GNP *(1 point)*
   From table 7.4 from Case & Fair we see

   GNP = GDP + Receipts of factor income from the rest of the world − Payments of factor income to the rest of the world

   = 5758.5 + 121.6 − 128.4 = **5751.7**.

   C. Calculate NNP *(1 point)*
   NNP = GNP − Depreciation = 5751.7 − 610.5 = **5141.2**.

2. A. Calculate Gross Investment *(3 Points)*
   Using the expenditure approach (table 7.2 from Case & Fair), we have

   GDP = C + I + G + (Ex − Im) = [Durable goods + Non durable goods + Services] + **Gross investment** + Government spending + Net exports

   = [1252 + 507.1 + 2083.4] + Gross investment + 1076.2 + (748.3 − 705.9)

   = 4961.1 + **Gross investment**.

   Use the GNP figure we obtained from (1) to get

   5751.7 = 4961.1 + **Gross investment**

   which gives, **Gross investment = 797.4**.

B. Calculate Net Investment *(1 Point)*
Net investment = Gross investment − Depreciation = 797.4 − 610.5 = **186.9**.

3. A. Calculate Personal Income *(2 points)*
   From page 153 in Case & Fair we see

   Personal income = NNP − Indirect taxes minus subsidies − Corporate profits minus dividends − Social insurance payments + Personal interest income + Transfer payments

   = 5141.2 − (522.4 − 40.1) − (321.5 − 40.8) − 511.1 + 221.3 + 733.4

   = **4821.8**.

   B. Calculate Disposable Income *(1 point)*
   By table 7.5 from Case & Fair we have

   Disposable income = Personal income − Personal taxes = 4821.8 − 705.7

   = **4116.1**.

TEST 5

DIRECTIONS: Each question or incomplete statement is followed by several suggested answers or completions. Select the one that BEST answers the question or completes the statement. *PRINT THE LETTER OF THE CORRECT ANSWER IN THE SPACE AT THE RIGHT.*

1. If income rises from $600 to $700 and consumption rises from $300 to $380, the marginal propensity to consume is

    (a) 0.54
    (b) 0.80
    (c) 1.00
    (d) 0.65

2. If Total Expenditures exceeds Total Production at the current level of real GDP

    (a) inventories will build up above desired levels, so firms will cut production.
    (b) inventories will fall below desired levels, so firms will cut production.
    (c) inventories will build up above desired levels, so firms will increase production.
    (d) inventories will fall below desired levels, so firms will increase production.

3. The government wishes to reduce total income by $80 billion. If the Keynesian multiplier for government spending is 2, what is the decrease in government purchases of goods and services that would do the job:

    (a) $20 billion
    (b) $40 billion
    (c) $80 billion
    (d) We don't have enough information

4. **Refer to the figure below.**
    This household's saving will be zero when income is

    (a) $400
    (b) $800
    (c) $1,000
    (d) $1,800

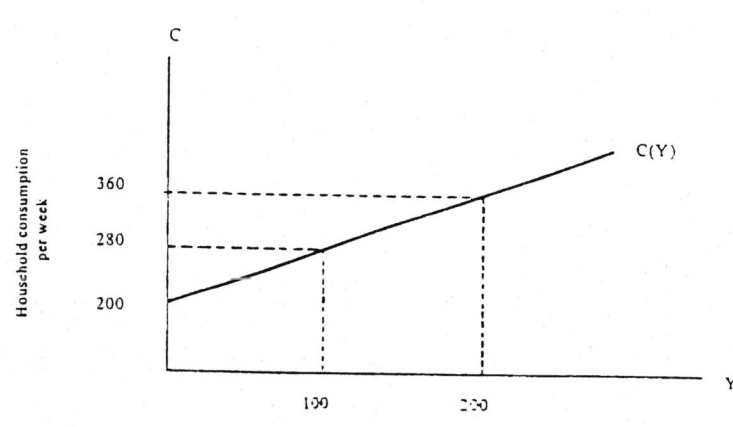

5. Assume an economy with no exports and no imports, in which consumers always spend $20 billion PLUS 50% of their after-tax income, or

$$C = 20 + 0.5(Y-TX),$$

investors always want to invest $120 billion, or

$$I = \bar{I} = 120,$$

and the government has a balanced budget of $80 billion, or

$$G = 80 = TX.$$

(a) What is the equilibrium level of national income (Y_1)? (Show your work.)

(b) Due to optimistic business expectations, investment spending increases by $30 billion, or now investment is

$$I = \bar{I} = 150.$$

Assume everything else remains the same.

Compute the new equilibrium level of national income (Y_2). (Show your work)

(c) Now suppose the government believes that this increase in investment spending (to $150 billion) may bring inflationary pressures. To combat this inflationary threat, the government raises taxes by $20 billion. Assume that the **government still has a balanced budget** so that now

$$G = 100 = TX.$$

(i) Using a circular flow diagram to derive the resulting changes in income, show how income will *fall or rise* as a result of this change in government fiscal policy. (Show your work for at least 3 successive changes in income.)

What will be the new equilibrium level of income (Y_3)?

(ii) What is the Keynesian multiplier for this change in taxes when the budget is balanced?

KEY (CORRECT ANSWERS)

1. (b) (1 pt.)
2. (d) (1 pt.)
3. (b) (1 pt.)
4. (c) (1 pt.)

$S = Y - C$, where S = household savings, Y = Income, C = Consumption.

This household's savings is zero, so

$0 = Y - C$ or,

$Y = C$.

From the information given on the graph, we find that the consumption function is,

$C = 200 + 0.8Y$.

→ $Y = 200 + 0.8Y$ since $C = Y$

→ $Y = 1000$

5.(a) (1 pt.)

$Y_1 = C + I + G$

Plugging in,

$Y_1 = 20 + 0.5(Y_1 - 80) + 120 + 80$

→ $Y_1 = 0.5Y_1 + 180$

→ $0.5Y_1 = 180$

→ $Y_1 = 360$

(b) (2 pts.)

$\Delta I = 30$

$$\rightarrow \Delta Y = \Delta I \left(\frac{1}{1 - MPC} \right)$$

$$= 30 \left(\frac{1}{0.5} \right) \quad \text{since MPC} = 0.5$$

$$= 60$$

So the new equilibrium level of national income is,

$$Y_2 = 360 + 60$$

$$= 420$$

An alternative solution would be to solve

$$Y_2 = C + I_2 + G$$

$$= 20 + 0.5(Y_2 - 80) + 150 + 80,$$

which also gives $Y_2 = 420$.

(c) (i) (2 pts.)

The first three rounds of changes in income when taxes change:

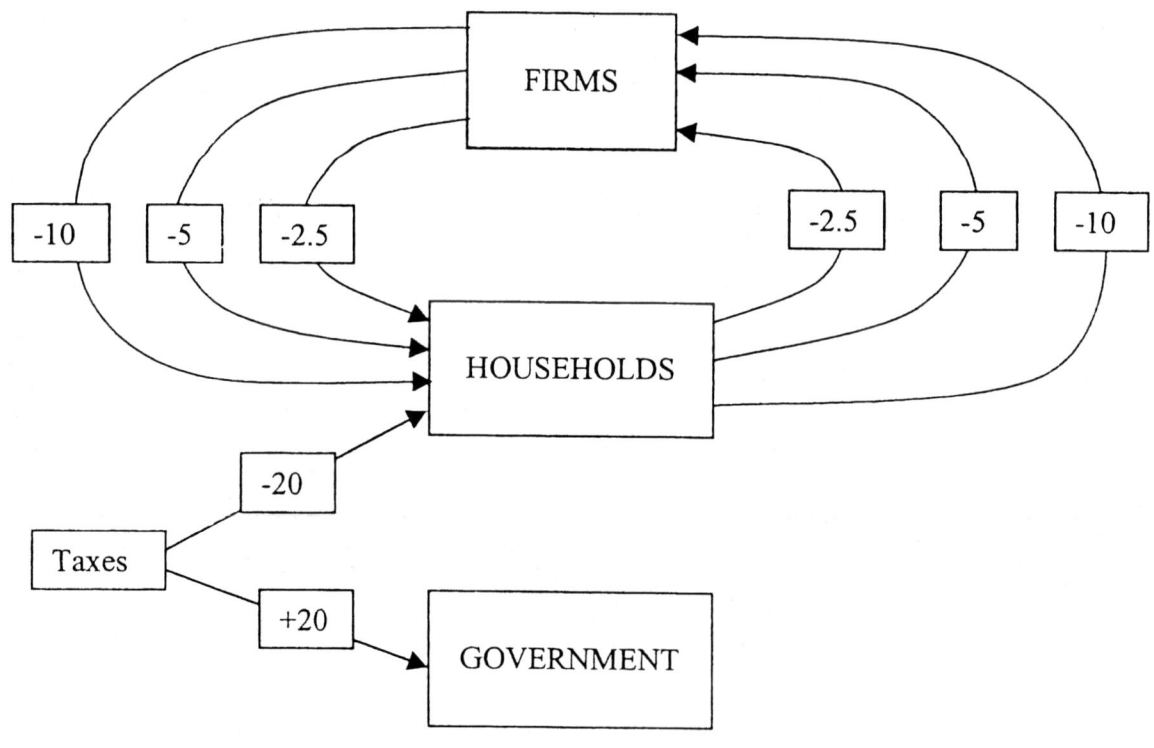

The first three rounds of changes in income when government spending changes:

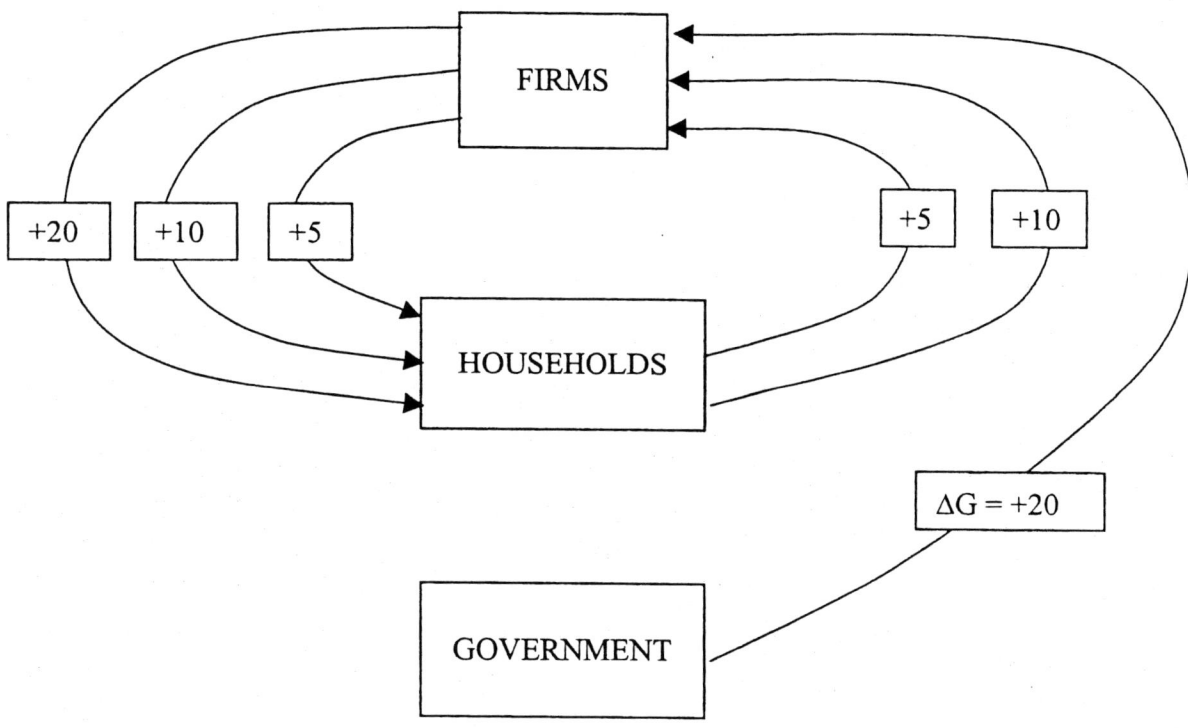

As a result of change in taxes,

$$\Delta Y = \Delta TX\left(\frac{-MPC}{1-MPC}\right)$$

$\rightarrow \quad \Delta Y = 20\left(\frac{-0.5}{0.5}\right)$

$\quad = -20$

As a result of change in government spending,

$$\Delta Y = \Delta G\left(\frac{1}{1-MPC}\right)$$

$\rightarrow \quad \Delta Y = 20\left(\frac{1}{0.5}\right)$

$\quad = 40$

Total change in Y = 40 − 20 = +20

Therefore,

$$Y_3 = 420 + 20$$

$$= 440$$

(c) (ii) (1 pt.)

The combined multiplier for any simultaneous change in G and TX is:

$$\Delta Y = \Delta G \left(\frac{1}{1 - MPC} \right) + \Delta TX \left(\frac{-MPC}{1 - MPC} \right). \quad (1)$$

If the budget is balanced, then

$$G = TX,$$

and $\Delta G = \Delta TX.$ (2)

Substituting ΔTX for ΔG in (1) gives

$$\Delta Y = \Delta TX \left(\frac{1}{1 - MPC} \right) + \Delta TX \left(\frac{-MPC}{1 - MPC} \right)$$

$$= \frac{\Delta TX \, (1 - MPC)}{(1 - MPC)}$$

$$= \Delta TX \times (1).$$

So the Keynesian multiplier is 1.

TEST 6

DIRECTIONS: Each question or incomplete statement is followed by several suggested answers or completions. Select the one that BEST answers the question or completes the statement. *PRINT THE LETTER OF THE CORRECT ANSWER IN THE SPACE AT THE RIGHT.*

This exercise is on the multiple contraction of the money supply resulting from the Open Market Sales of securities by the Federal Reserve. Assume:
 (a) the reserve requirement of commercial banks is 10%,
 (b) For questions 1-4, all commercial banks hold **no** excess reserves.

1. Suppose the Federal Reserve sells two $20,000 bonds, one each to Burt and Ernie. Burt pays for his bond with money he withdraws from his account at Key Bank. Ernie pays for his bond with money he has kept hidden in his garbage can.

    (a) The following is Key Bank's balance sheet **before** Burt withdraws $20,000 in cash. Complete the balance sheet.

    Key Bank: Balance Sheet

Assets		Liabilities	
Reserves	_____	Demand Deposits:	
Loans	_____	of Burt	_____
Securities	100,000	of others	600,000
Total	650,000	Total	_____

    (b) On the balance sheet below, show the impact on Key Bank's balance sheet of Burt's withdrawal of cash.

    Key Bank: Balance Sheet

Assets		Liabilities	
Reserves	_____	Demand Deposits:	
Loans	_____	of Burt	_____
Securities	_____	of others	_____
Total	_____	Total	_____

    (c) By how much do Key Bank's reserves fall short of the legal requirement?
    _____

2. Suppose Key Bank replenishes its reserves by selling some of its securities to Oscar (i.e., the bank sells Oscar securities equal to the amount its reserves fall short). Oscar has a demand deposit at Big Bird Bank.

   (a) Complete Big Bird Bank's balance sheet **before** Oscar's purchase.

   Big Bird Bank: Balance Sheet

Assets		Liabilities	
Reserves	_____	Demand Deposits:	
Loans	425,000	of Oscar	128,000
Securities	_____	of others	537,000
Total	_____	Total	_____

   (b) Show what happens on Key Bank's balance sheet when Oscar pays for those securities by giving Key Bank a personal check on his deposit at Big Bird Bank, which Key Bank turns over to Big Bird Bank in exchange for cash.

   Key Bank: Balance Sheet

Assets		Liabilities	
Reserves	_____	Demand Deposits:	
Loans	_____	of Burt	_____
Securities	_____	of others	_____
Total	_____	Total	_____

3. What is the decrease in money supply so far, due only to the original sale of two bonds to Burt and Ernie as well as the subsequent sale of Key Bank securities to Oscar? (Hint: A decrease in the money supply includes a decrease in dollar bills in circulation as well as a decrease in demand deposits.)

   _____

4. (a) If Big Bird Bank replenishes its shortage of reserves (caused by transactions described in question 2) by selling some of its securities, how much must it sell?

   _____

   (b) What will be the ultimate decrease in the money supply resulting from the sale of the two bonds to Burt and Ernie?

   _____

5. Suppose that, **before the sale of bonds to Burt and Ernie,** all banks became nervous about the East Asian financial crisis and were not eager to lend money. Although the legal reserve requirement stayed at 10%, banks now insist on always holding 20% of demand deposits in reserves.

   (a) If the total demand deposits of these two banks are those indicated above in 1(a) (for Key Bank) and 2(a) (for Big Bird Bank), what would be the total reserves held by Key Bank and Big Bird Bank (i.e., the sum of both sets of reserves)?

   _____

   (b) Now assume the sale of bonds to Burt and Ernie take place as described previously. What will be the ultimate decrease in the money supply resulting from the sale of these two bonds?

   _____

KEY (CORRECT ANSWERS)

1. (a) (1 point) Remembering bank assets always equal bank liabilities and noting that Key Bank will only hold the legal limit of reserves, Key Bank's initial balance sheet reads as follows (required answers in bold):

Key Bank: Balance Sheet

Assets		Liabilities	
Reserves	**65,000**	Demand Deposits:	
Loans	**485,000**	of Burt	50,000
Securities	100,000	of others	600,000
Total	650,000	Total	650,000

(b) (1 point) When Burt withdraws $20,000 in cash, the cash the bank has on hand (i.e. reserves) also falls by $20,000.

Key Bank: Balance Sheet

Assets		Liabilities	
Reserves	**45,000**	Demand Deposits:	
Loans	**485,000**	of Burt	30,000
Securities	100,000	of others	600,000
Total	630,000	Total	630,000

(c) (1 point) The legal reserve requirement is $630,000 \times 0.1 = \$63,000$. Key Bank's current reserves are $45,000. Therefore, Key Bank's reserves are $63,000 - $45,000 = $18,000 short of the legal requirement.

2. (a) (1 point) Using the same concepts as in question 1(a), Big Bird Bank's balance sheet **before** Oscar's purchase was:

Big Bird Bank: Balance Sheet

Assets		Liabilities	
Reserves	**66,500**	Demand Deposits:	
Loans	425,000	of Oscar	128,000
Securities	**173,500**	of others	537,000
Total	665,000	Total	665,000

(b) (1 point) After Key Bank sells $18,000 in securities to Oscar and receives the cash (via Big Bird Bank), its balance sheet is as follows:

Key Bank: Balance Sheet

Assets		Liabilities	
Reserves	63,000	Demand Deposits:	
Loans	485,000	of Burt	30,000
Securities	82,000	of others	600,000
Total	630,000	Total	630,000

3. (1 point) A decrease in the money supply includes a decrease in dollar bills in the hands of people as well as a decrease in demand deposits. The $20,000 in bills taken from Ernie simply came from his garbage can. When Burt took his $20,000 from the bank, he lowered his demand deposits by $20,000. This withdrawal had the additional effect of forcing the bank to increase its cash on hand (reserves). It responded by selling a security which, in turn, caused Oscar's demand deposits to decrease by $18,000. Therefore, the total decrease in the money supply so far is $58,000.

4. (a) (1 point) When Oscar takes out $18,000 from Big Bird Bank, the bank's demand deposits are now $665,000 - $18,000 = $647,000. So, the legal reserve requirement is $647,000 × 0.1 = $64,700. On the other hand, the bank's reserves are $66,500 - $18,000 = $48,500. Since Big Bird Bank is short of the requirement by the amount of $64,700 - $48,500 = $16,200, it will be forced to sell $16,200 worth of securities to replenish the shortage of reserves (caused by transactions described in question 2).

(b) (1 point) The ultimate decrease in the money supply resulting from the sale of the two bonds to Burt and Ernie will be $220,000. The decrease is the sum of the decrease of $20,000 as a result of Ernie paying in dollar bills and the eventual decrease in the money supply caused by Burt's payment of $20,000. Since the required reserve ratio is 0.1, the money multiplier is $\left(\dfrac{1}{0.1}\right) = 10$ and Burt's payment of $20,000 induces a decrease of 20,000 × 10 = $200,000 in the money supply.

5. If all banks <u>always</u> hold 20% of demand deposits in reserves, then the legal limit of 10% has no bearing. We know that banks will keep cash equal to 20 percent of their demand deposits. Therefore before the sale of bonds to Burt and Ernie:

(a) (1 point) The reserves held by Key Bank is $650,000 × 0.2 = $130,000 and the reserves held by Big Bird Bank is $665,000 × 0.2 = $133,000. So, the total reserves held by both banks is $130,000 + $133,000 = $263,000.

(b) (1 point) If the sale of bonds to Burt and Ernie take place as described previously, the <u>ultimate</u> decrease in the money supply resulting from the sale of these two bonds will be $120,000. There is a loss of $20,000 in dollar bills that Ernie used to hold. Additionally, there is a loss of $20,000 in reserves to the banking system. The effective reserve ratio is 20% so our multiplier is now $\left(\dfrac{1}{0.2}\right) = 5$, which means that the resulting decrease in the money supply from Burt's withdrawal is $20,000 \times 5 = 100,000$. Adding up, we calculate the ultimate decrease in the money supply to be $20,000 + \$100,000 = \$120,000$.

TEST 7

DIRECTIONS: Each question or incomplete statement is followed by several suggested answers or completions. Select the one that BEST answers the question or completes the statement. *PRINT THE LETTER OF THE CORRECT ANSWER IN THE SPACE AT THE RIGHT.*

1. As interest rates rise,

    a. the money demand curve will shift to the right.
    b. people are discouraged from buying bonds.
    c. people are discouraged from moving out of bonds and into money.
    d. the money supply curve will shift to the right.

2. If the demand curve for investment is very steep (rather than flat), the result will be

    a. a very effective monetary policy
    b. a very ineffective monetary policy.
    c. a very ineffective fiscal policy.
    d. great instability in bank reserves.
    e. a very stable interest rate.

3. An increase in the level of national income (Y) combined with the sale of government securities by the Federal Reserve will have what effect on the equilibrium interest rate?

    a. an increase in the interest rate.
    b. a decrease in the interest rate.
    c. no effect on the interest rate.
    d. an indeterminate effect on the interest rate.

4. Landia has a small economy with only one firm, Landcorp. Landcorp is an agricultural firm facing four alternative projects to invest in, as summarized below.

Project	Cost ($ millions)	Expected Rate of Return (%)
Worker Education	40	7
Inventory Speculation	10	9
New Tractors	60	5
New Silo	140	3

The demand for new housing in Landia is related to the interest rate in the following way:

Interest rate (%)	Investment in Residential Construction ($ millions)
10	10
8	20
6	30
4	40
2	50

a. Draw the demand curve for investment for the economy of Landia.

b. Assume that Landia does not have any foreign trade. Consumers always spend $60 million plus 50% of the after-tax income, or

$$C = 60 + 0.5(Y - Tx).$$

Government spending is $100 million and taxes collected are $120 million, or

$$G = 100, Tx = 120.$$

If the equilibrium level of income is $500 million, what must be the total desired investment in this economy?

c. Given your answer to (b), can you calculate the equilibrium interest rate? If so, indicate the numerical value of that interest rate. If not, explain why it cannot be calculated.

KEY (CORRECT ANSWERS)

1. (1 point) The answer is (c).

2. (1 point) The answer is (b). Refer to the figure below.

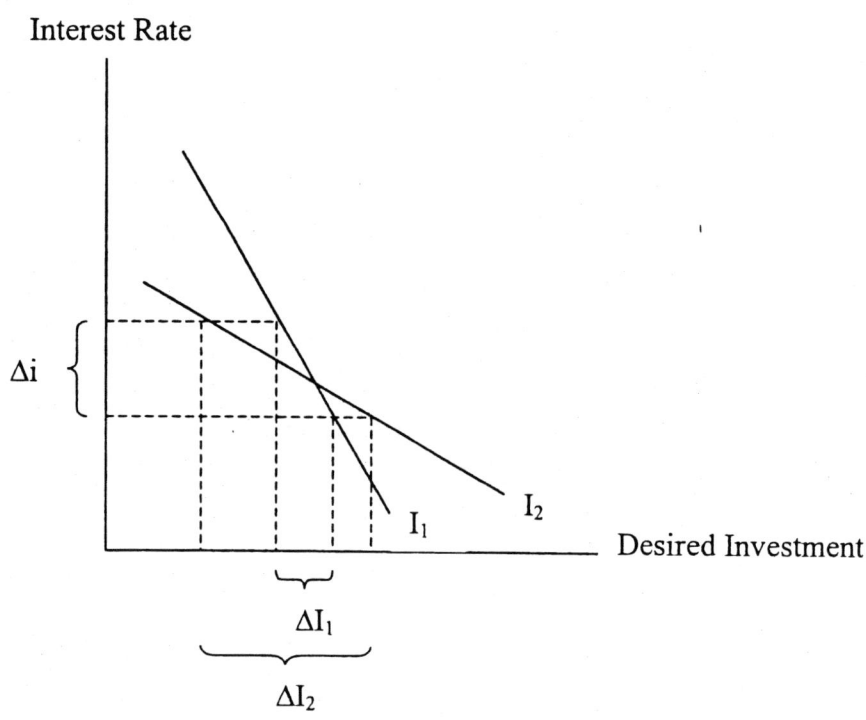

Monetary policy works through the interest rate. The steeper the demand curve for investment (I_1 is steeper than I_2), the smaller is the change in investment spending ($\Delta I_1 < \Delta I_2$) induced by a given change in the interest rate (Δi).

3. (2 points) The answer is (a). Using causal arrows, the impact of the increase in the level of national income on the equilibrium interest rate is

   $+ \Delta Y \rightarrow + \Delta LP(T) \rightarrow + \Delta i$.

   On the other hand, sale of government securities by the Federal Reserve contracts the money supply and the impact of the contraction on the equilibrium interest rate is

   $- \Delta M \rightarrow + \Delta i$.

   Since both effects are in the same direction, the final effect is unambiguous.

4. a. (3 points) As the market interest rate gets lower (the opportunity cost decreases), more and more projects become worth undertaking, as summarized below.

Interest Rate(%)	Projects Worth Undertaking	Non-Residential I ($ millions)	Residential I ($ millions)	Total I ($ millions)
10	None	0	10	10
8	Inventory Speculation	10	20	30
6	Inventory Speculation, Worker Education	50	30	80
4	Inventory Speculation, Worker Education, New Tractors	110	40	150
2	All	250	50	300

The data in the table suggests the following demand curve for investment:

The Demand Curve for Investment

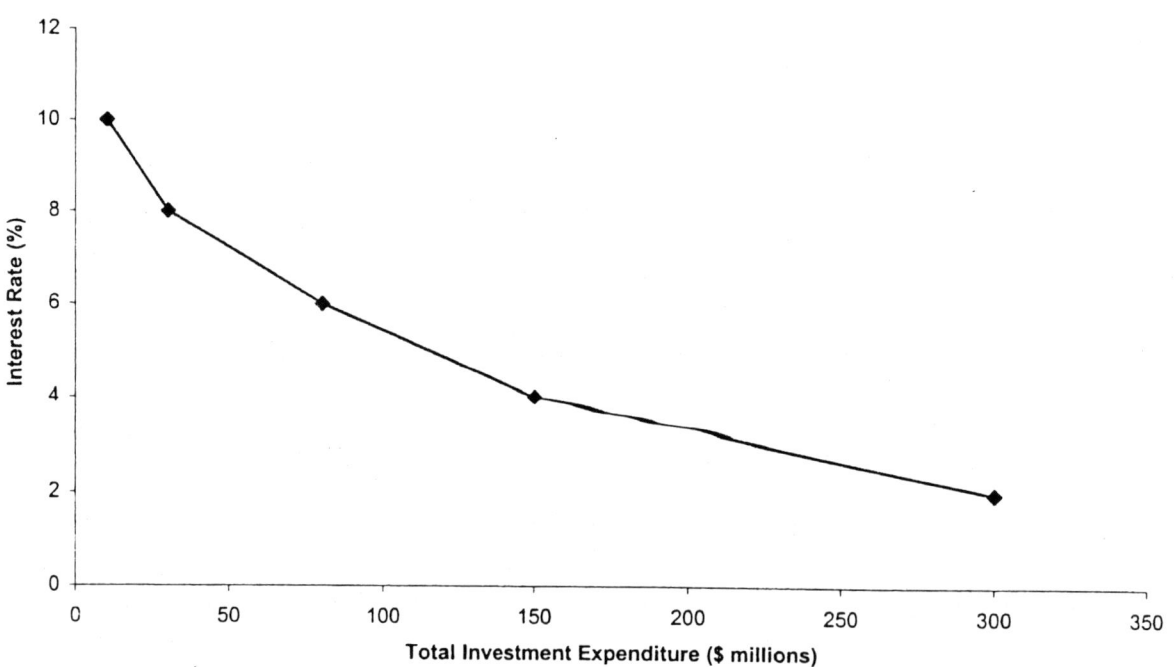

b. (2 points) We use the equilibrium condition for national income to figure out the level of desired investment.

$$Y = C + I + G$$
$$= 60 + 0.5(Y - 120) + I + 100$$
$$= 60 + 0.5(500 - 120) + I + 100$$
$$= 500.$$

$\Rightarrow I = 150.$

c. (1 point) From the graph of the demand curve for investment, we can see that the equilibrium interest rate is 4 %.

TEST 8

DIRECTIONS: Each question or incomplete statement is followed by several suggested answers or completions. Select the one that BEST answers the question or completes the statement. *PRINT THE LETTER OF THE CORRECT ANSWER IN THE SPACE AT THE RIGHT.*

1. In June there are 5,000 people classified as unemployed and the size of the labor force is 100,000. The only change between June and July is that 1,000 people give up looking for work. Which of the following is true?

   a. In June the unemployment rate was 5% and in July the unemployment rate was 4%.
   b. The unemployment rate in both June and July was 5%.
   c. In June the unemployment rate was 4.8% and in July the unemployment rate was 4%.
   d. In June the unemployment rate was 5% and in July the unemployment rate was 4.04%.

2. The decrease in the demand for mainframe computers caused manufacturers of mainframe computers to reduce prices by 20%. This is an example of

   a. inflation.
   b. deflation.
   c. a sustained inflation.
   d. the operations of supply and demand.

	Units consumed	Price in Period 1	Price in Period 2	Price in Period 3
Good A	4	$1.00	$1.50	$2.00
Good B	10	$1.50	$2.00	$2.00
Good C	6	$2.00	$2.50	$3.00

3. **Refer to the table above.** If period 1 is the base period, the inflation rate between period 2 and period 3 is approximately

   a. 10.88.
   b. 12.2.
   c. 16.14.
   d. 39.37.

4. Assume that The Republic of Flutie does not trade with foreign countries. Consumers always spend $175 million plus 50% of after-tax income, or

$$C = 175 + 0.5(Y - TX). \quad \ldots \quad (1)$$

Desired investment (I) varies inversely with the interest rate (i), in the following way:

$$I = 1000 - 8000(i). \quad \ldots \quad (2)$$

That is, if the interest rate is 5%, investors want to invest $1000 million minus 5% of $8000 million (which is $400 million). Note that an interest rate of 5% translates to i = 0.05.

Currently, the government spends $100 million and taxes $150 million, or

$$G = 100, \quad TX = 150.$$

The total money demand (M_D) in this economy varies inversely with the interest rate such that

$$M_D = 1500 - 10000(i). \quad \ldots \quad (3)$$

That is, if the interest rate is 5%, total money demand is $1500 million minus 5% of $10,000 million (which is $500 million).

The current money supply (M_S) is $500 million, or

$$M_S = 500. \quad \ldots \quad (4)$$

a. What is the equilibrium interest rate? (Hint: equilibrium occurs where supply equals demand.)
b. At that equilibrium interest rate what is the level of desired investment?
c. What is the equilibrium level of national income?
d. Due to the economic crisis in Japan, the investors in this economy change their investment behavior such that now they want to invest $300 million regardless of what the interest rate is. That is, equation (2) above is now replaced with

$$I = \bar{I} = 200. \quad \ldots \quad (2A)$$

Wade Phillips, the president of The Republic of Flutie, announces that he will stimulate the economy by increasing the money supply from $500 million to $700 million. Will his action be able to increase national income above the previous level (your answer to (c))?

KEY (CORRECT ANSWERS)

1. (2 points) The answer is (d). First, recall that (see p. 172 in the text)

$$\text{Unemployment rate} = \frac{\text{Unemployed}}{\text{Labor Force}}.$$

In June, the labor force was 100,000 and the unemployed was 5000 which gives

$$\text{Unemployment rate in June} = \frac{5000}{100,000} = 0.05, \text{ or } 5\%.$$

In July, when 1000 people stop looking for work, the unemployed goes down by 1000. Since *people who are not looking for work are not in the labor force*, the labor force decreases by 1000 as well (see p.172). Consequently, we obtain

$$\text{Unemployment rate in July} = \frac{4000}{99,000} = 0.04040404 \cdots, \text{ or approximately}$$

4.04%.

2. (1 point) The answer is (d). There is a decrease in the price of mainframe computers, but that is not deflation. That is because the decrease in not in the *overall price level*, but in the price of one commodity only (see p. 179 in the text). What is happening can be explained by using the supply-and-demand analysis. As demand for mainframe computers decreases from D_0 to D_1, there is a drop in the equilibrium price from p_0 to p_1 (assume this is a 20% decrease).

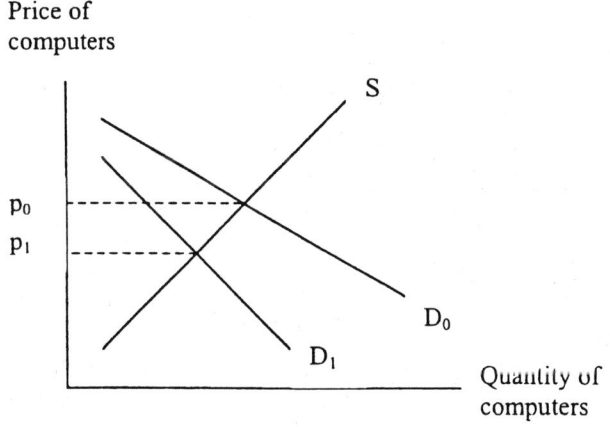

3. (1 point) The answer is (b). **See p. 161 in the text**. The bundle price in period t (where t can be 1, 2 or 3) is

(units consumed of good A × price of good A in period t) + (units consumed of good B × price of good B in period t) + (units consumed of good B × price of good B in period t)

and the price index in period 2 is

$$\text{Index (2)} = \frac{\text{Bundle price in period 2}}{\text{Bundle price in base period}} \times 100.$$

The index for period 3 is defined similarly. Then the inflation rate between period 2 and period 3 is

$$\frac{\text{Index (3)} - \text{Index (2)}}{\text{Index (2)}} \times 100.$$

Since we are told that the base period is period 1, we compute

$$\text{Index (2)} = \frac{(4 \times 1.5) + (10 \times 2) + (6 \times 2.5)}{(4 \times 1) + (10 \times 1.5) + (6 \times 2)} \times 100 = \frac{41}{31} \times 100 = 132.26$$

and

$$\text{Index (3)} = \frac{(4 \times 2) + (10 \times 2) + (6 \times 3)}{(4 \times 1) + (10 \times 1.5) + (6 \times 2)} \times 100 = \frac{46}{31} \times 100 = 148.39.$$

Hence the inflation rate between period 2 and period 3 is

$$\frac{148.39 - 132.26}{132.26} \times 100 = 12.1957 \approx 12.2.$$

4. a. (1 point) Setting $M_D = M_S$ gives

$$1500 - 10{,}000(i) = 500$$

$$1000 = 10{,}000(i)$$

$$i = 0.1, \text{ or } 10\%.$$

b. (1 point) When the interest rate is 10%, desired investment is

$$I = 1000 - 8000(0.1)$$
$$= 200.$$

c. (2 points) Once we know the desired level of investment, we can figure out the equilibrium level of national income

$$Y = C + I + G$$
$$= 175 + 0.5(Y - 150) + 200 + 100$$
$$= 175 + 0.5Y - 75 + 200 + 100$$
$$0.5Y = 400$$
$$Y = 800.$$

d. (2 points) Now that desired investment is always $200 million, our computation for the <u>initial</u> level of equilibrium Y is exactly the same as in (c), $800 million. What happens to equilibrium income as the money supply is increased from $500 million to $700 million? The answer is, *nothing*. See the figure below.

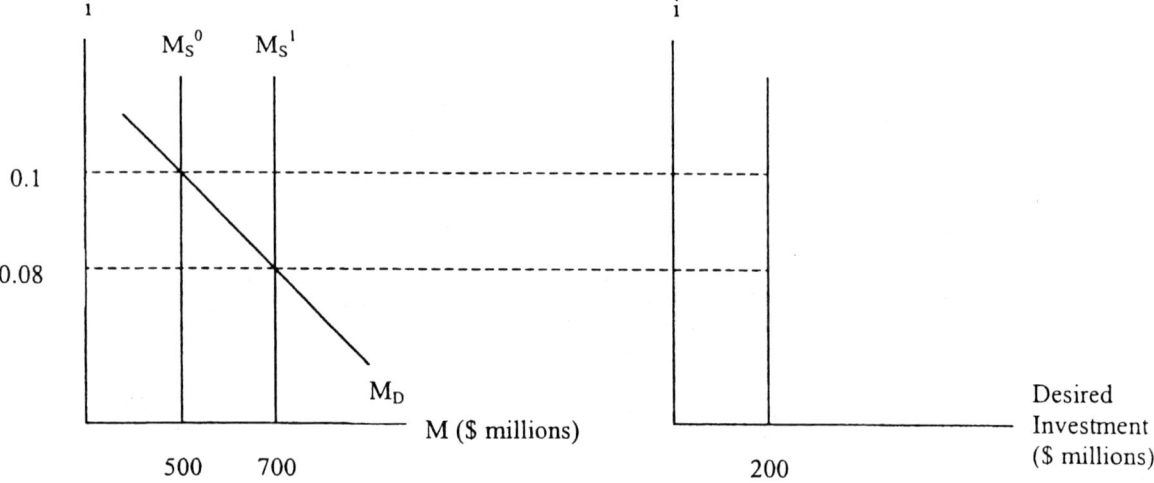

As the money supply increases from M_S^0 to M_S^1, the equilibrium interest rate drops from 10% to 8% (as seen by setting $M_D = M_S$ with the new money supply of $700 million). However, since desired investment no longer depends on the interest rate, the drop from 10% to 8% fails to increase desired investment. Consequently, the equilibrium level of income is still $800 million after the increase in the money supply.

For those who did not realize the typo and used $300 million as the desired investment figure, the equilibrium level of income is computed to be

$$Y = C + I + G$$

$$= 175 + 0.5(Y - 150) + 300 + 100$$

$$= 175 + 0.5Y - 75 + 300 + 100$$

$$0.5Y = 500$$

$$Y = 1000.$$

So the answer is, equilibrium income increases from $800 million to $1000 million as a result of the increase in desired investment. But, **this increase is not due to the increase in the money supply**. Monetary policy is ineffective due to the same reason explained at the beginning of (d). So, the answer does not change in the sense that the action of Wade Phillips does not increase equilibrium income above the old equilibrium level of income of $800 million, but the increase in desired investment does.

TEST 9

DIRECTIONS: Each question or incomplete statement is followed by several suggested answers or completions. Select the one that BEST answers the question or completes the statement. *PRINT THE LETTER OF THE CORRECT ANSWER IN THE SPACE AT THE RIGHT.*

1. Which of the following does not increase real output per manhour?

   a. Education.
   b. Growth in output.
   c. Innovation.
   d. Economies of scale.
   e. All of the above can increase real output per manhour.

2. The increased defense spending that marked the late 1960s produced

   a. cost-push inflation.
   b. demand-pull inflation.
   c. a sudden reduction in the rate of inflation caused by a rise in interest rates.
   d. dramatically higher unemployment as military projects took resources away from civilian employment projects.
   e. none of the above.

3. **Refer to the figure below.**

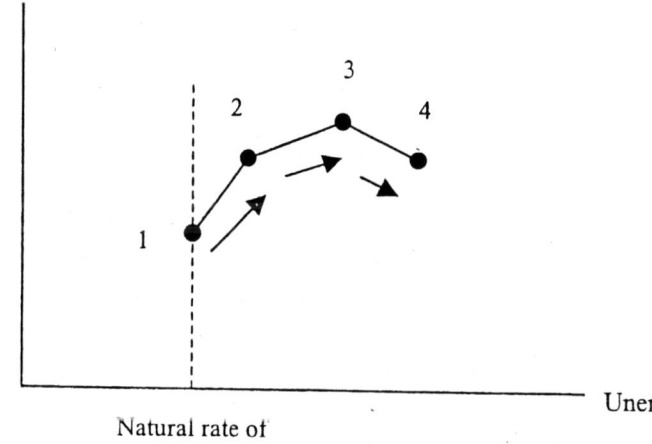

The dots indicate positions during a 4-year cycle (i.e. dot 1 is the year 1 position, dot 2 is the year 2 position, etc.) and the arrows indicate movement from one year to the next. The cycle represented by movement along the arrows shown in the figure is most appropriately associated with

a. an economic boom.
b. a recession caused by a supply-side price shock.
c. a recession caused by contractionary fiscal policy.
d. an economic expansion caused by an expansionary monetary policy.
e. a recovery fueled by a reduction in saving.

4. Assume in a simple economy GDP or output (O) is a simple function of existing capital stock (K), such that the output created during a given year t is always equal to five times the value of the capital stock, or

$$O_t = 5K_t.$$

Notice that saving in year t must equal investment in year t, and the latter equals the increment to capital stock in year t, or

$$K_{t+1} - K_t = \Delta K = I_t = S_t.$$

Assume there is <u>no depreciation</u>. You are given the following information:

Year	S_t	I_t	K_t	O_t	ΔO	$\Delta O/O_t$
1990	50	50	100	500	-	-
1991	50	50	150	750	250	0.333333
1992	40					
1993	35					
1994	30					
1995	20					
1996	15					
1997	10					

a. Complete the entries of the table.
b. Over time, what is happening to the rate of saving (the ratio of savings divided by output, or S_t/O_t)?
c. What is happening to the output growth rate ($\Delta O/O_t$) over time?
d. What is the linkage between the change in the saving rate (your answer to (b)) and the change in the output growth rate (your answer to (c))? Explain using a production possibilities curve. (Hint: see p. 143 in the *Guide*.)

KEY (CORRECT ANSWERS)

1. (1 point) The answer is (b). Growth in output does not increase real output per manhour. Choice (e) is also acceptable if constant population and growth occurs although it does not offer ant explanation to why growth occurred in the first place.

2. (1 point) The answer is (b). Increased defense spending increased demand, causing inflation.

3. (2 points) The answer is (b). Since inflation and unemployment are going up at the same time, we are in some sort of a recession not a boom. A contractionary fiscal policy would have reduced inflation from the start.

4. a. (2 points) We use the relationships

    $I_t = S_t$

    $K_{t+1} = K_t + I_t$

    and

    $O_t = 5K_t$

    to compute the entries of the table. The completed table looks like the following (completed entries in bold):

Year	S_t	I_t	K_t	O_t	ΔO	$\Delta O/O_t$
1990	50	50	100	500	-	-
1991	50	50	150	750	250	0.333333
1992	40	40	200	1000	250	0.25
1993	35	35	240	1200	200	0.166667
1994	30	30	275	1375	175	0.127273
1995	20	20	305	1525	150	0.098361
1996	15	15	325	1625	100	0.061538
1997	10	10	340	1700	75	0.044118

   b. and c. (2 points, 1 point each) The saving rate and the output growth rate through time can be summarized by the following table:

Year	S_t/O_t	$\Delta O_t/O_t$
1990	0.1	-
1991	0.066667	0.333333
1992	0.04	0.25
1993	0.029167	0.166667
1994	0.021818	0.127273
1995	0.013115	0.098361
1996	0.009231	0.061538
1997	0.005882	0.044118

We see that the saving rate and the output growth rate are both decreasing over time. See the graph below.

Notation: $\Delta O/O$ = DO/O = output growth rate and S/O = saving rate.

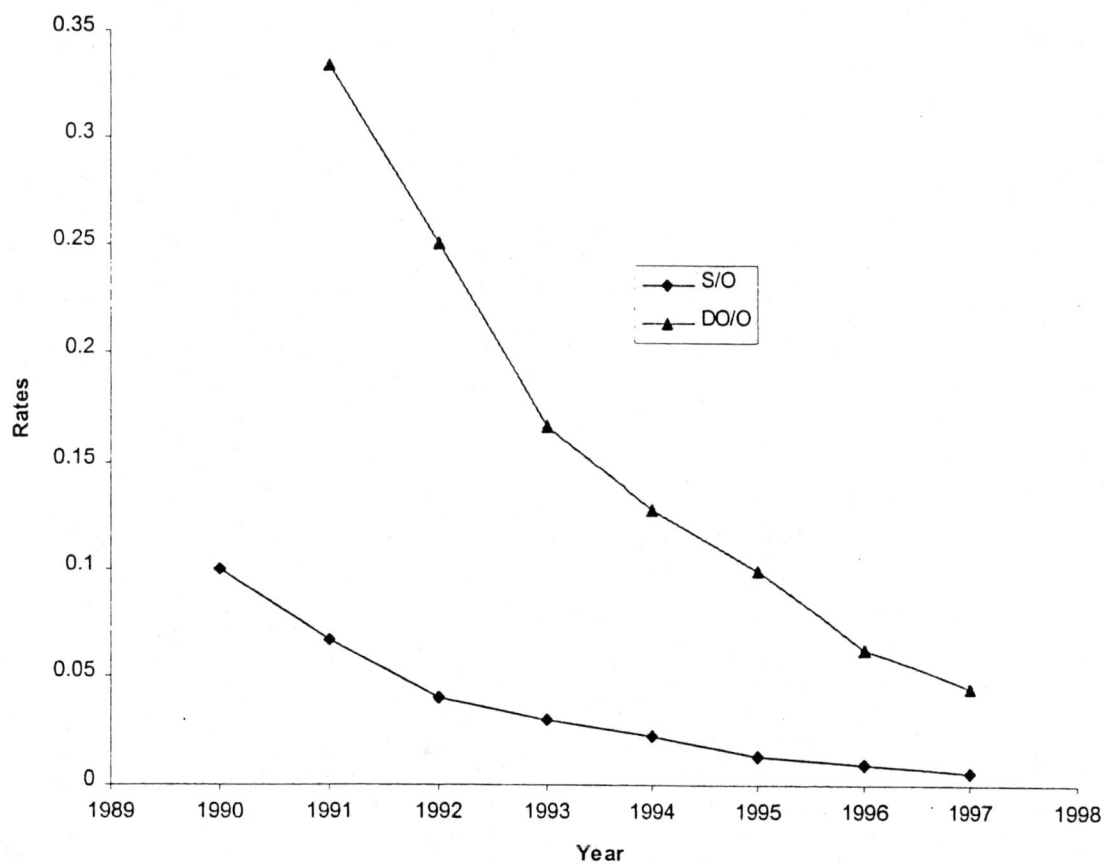

d. (2 points) We see that the saving rate and the output growth rate move in the same direction through time. Let's explain this phenomenon with a PPF as done in class. We can consider the economy having two kinds of goods, consumption goods and investment goods.

If a society consumes more, it is saves less and invests less. Since investment is essential to growth, societies that invest more experience more growth.

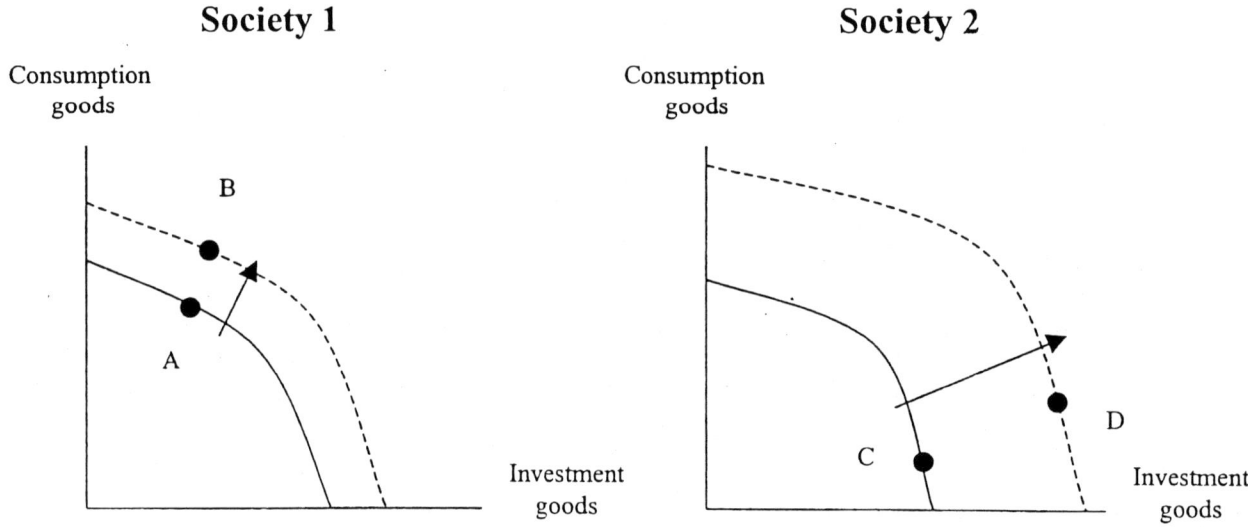

While society 1 experiences growth (moves from A to B), society 2 experiences even greater growth (moves from C to D) because it invests more relative to society 1. That is what we see in the completed table of (a) - as saving rates fall, investment decreases and growth rates fall.

TEST 10

1. Which of the following would NOT shift the demand curve for beef to a new position?
    a. a rise in the price of pork.
    b. a fall in the price of beef.
    c. an increase in the income of beef consumers.
    d. a widespread advertising campaign undertaken by the producers of a product competitive with beef.
    e. a change in people's tastes with respect to beef.

2. On the basis of Keynesian model of income determination, GDP is in equilibrium:
    a. whenever there is full employment.
    b. only if the marginal propensity to consume is equal to investment.
    c. whenever there is full employment without government interference.
    d. whenever desired saving equals desired (or planned) investment.
    e. whenever actual saving equals actual investment.

3. If the Keynesian investment multiplier is 2.5 and if investment rises by 20 while government spending falls by 10(other things being constant), by how much will the equilibrium level of income rise?
    a. 10.
    b. 25.
    c. 40.
    d. 50.
    e. 60.

4. Assuming a 15 percent required reserve ratio and a desire on the part of banks to keep 5 percent in excess reserves, a $100 cash deposit can result in a maximum increase in the money supply of:
    a. $100.
    b. $400.
    c. $500.
    d. $575.
    e. $675.

5. Which of the following is LEAST applicable to the concept of net domestic product (NDP)?
    a. a measure of output.
    b. the market value of final goods and services.
    c. the sum of all an economy's transactions involving money.
    d. a measure of income.
    e. GDP minus depreciation.

6. If a $200 million increase in investment results in a $600 million increase in overall consumption, what would be the result of a $200 million increase in government spending in this same economy?
   a. a $600 million increase in overall consumption.
   b. a decline in consumption of $600 million.
   c. a $400 million increase in overall consumption.
   d. a decline in consumption of $400 million.
   e. none of the above.

7. Which of the following will definitely lower the interest rate?
   a. open market purchases and an increase in the required reserve ratio.
   b. open market sales and an increase in the required reserve ratio.
   c. a decrease in the discount rate and an increase in the required reserve ratio.
   d. an increase in the discount rate and a decrease in the required reserve ratio.
   e. open market purchases and a decrease in the discount rate.

8. On the foreign exchange market, the demand curve for US dollars reflects all of the following EXCEPT:
   a. foreigners' desire to import our goods.
   b. their need to pay us dividends and interest payments.
   c. their desire to invest in our real estate.
   d. their desire to host us during our vacations.
   e. all of the above are reflected in the demand curve.

9. From the following table for a country with no exports and no imports, we know that:

GDP	Desired C	I	G
1,100	780	170	0
1,000	730	170	0
900	680	170	0
800	630	170	0
700	580	170	0

   a. when GDP is less than 750, actual investment is 170.
   b. when GDP is greater than 1,000, GDP will tend to rise.
   c. when GDP is 800, saving will equal 170.
   d. when GDP is less than 700, unwanted inventories will be accumulating.
   e. when GDP is 900, actual investment is less than 170.

10. Based on the following diagram, by how much must the government increase its spending in order to achieve full employment? (There is no foreign sector in this economy.)

a. 50   b. 100   c. 125   d. 150   e. 200

KEY (CORRECT ANSWERS)

Attention: *Each question is worth 1 point.*

1. The answer is (b). A fall in the price of beef will just induce a movement along the demand curve for beef.

2. The answer is (d). This is just the definition of equilibrium.

3. The answer is (b). First, recall that the government spending multiplier is equal to the investment multiplier which is 2.5. The net change in equilibrium income is

    $$\Delta Y = \text{multiplier} \times \Delta I + \text{multiplier} \times \Delta G$$
    $$= 2.5 \times 20 + 2.5 \times (-10)$$
    $$= 50 - 25$$
    $$= 25.$$

4. The answer is (c). Recall from problem set 6 that when banks are holding excess reserves, the money multiplier is

    $$\frac{1}{\text{required reserve ratio} + \text{excess reserve ratio}}.$$

    Then the maximum increase in the money supply is

    $$\Delta M = \left(\frac{1}{0.15 + 0.5}\right) \times \$100$$
    $$= \left(\frac{1}{0.20}\right) \times \$100$$
    $$= 5 \times \$100$$
    $$= \$500.$$

5. The answer is (c). There are a lot of illegal transactions involving money (e.g. drug trade) which *do not go through the market*. Those transactions are not part of NDP. Some other transactions involving money such as trading of stocks are not counted as part of NDP either.

6. The answer is (a). We know that

$$\Delta Y = \left(\frac{1}{1-\text{MPC}}\right) \times \Delta I. \qquad \ldots \quad (1)$$

We also know that the relationship between consumption and income is

$$C = a + bY.$$

Here b is the marginal propensity to consume. The above equation implies

$$\Delta C = \text{MPC} \times \Delta Y \qquad \ldots \quad (2)$$

since a is constant. Plugging (1) into (2) we see that a change in investment spending affects equilibrium consumption in the following way:

$$\Delta C = \text{MPC} \times \Delta Y$$

$$= \text{MPC} \times \left(\frac{1}{1-\text{MPC}}\right) \times \Delta I$$

$$= \left(\frac{\text{MPC}}{1-\text{MPC}}\right) \times \Delta I. \qquad \ldots \quad (3)$$

On the other hand, government spending and investment spending multipliers are the same, i.e.

$$\Delta Y = \left(\frac{1}{1-\text{MPC}}\right) \times \Delta G. \qquad \ldots \quad (4)$$

Plugging (4) into (2) gives

$$\Delta C = \left(\frac{\text{MPC}}{1-\text{MPC}}\right) \times \Delta G. \qquad \ldots \quad (5)$$

Comparing (3) and (5), we see that changes in investment spending and government spending affect consumption in exactly the same way. So since a $200 million increase in investment spending increases consumption by $600 million, a $200 million increase in government spending will increase consumption by $600 million as well.

7. The answer is (e). Open market purchases by the Federal Reserve increase the money supply, resulting in

$$+\Delta M \to -\Delta i.$$

On the other hand, a decrease in the discount rate causes banks to hold less excess reserves, increasing the money supply. Again, we obtain

$$+\Delta M \to -\Delta i.$$

Since the two effects are in the same direction, there is a definite decrease in the interest rate.

8. The answer is (d). When US citizens travel to foreign countries, they usually carry transactions with the currency of that country, <u>not with US dollars</u>. Therefore, foreigners do not demand US dollars for the purposes of hosting tourists from the US.

9. The answer is (c). Take a look at the following table.

GDP	C	GDP - C = Actual Investment
1100	780	320
1000	730	270
900	680	220
800	**630**	**170**
700	580	120

When GDP is 800, actual investment is equal to desired investment. So, 800 is an equilibrium level of GDP. We know that without government spending <u>in equilibrium</u>

$$Y = C + I. \quad \ldots \quad (1)$$

Without taxes, it is <u>always true</u> that

$$Y \equiv C + S. \quad \ldots \quad (2)$$

Plugging (1) in to (2), we see that <u>in equilibrium</u>

$$I = S,$$

or that saving is equal to desired investment of 170 when GDP is 800.

10. The answer is (b). To compute the government spending multiplier, we need to figure out what the marginal propensity to consume is. We know that the consumption function is of the form

$$C = a + bY, \qquad \ldots (1)$$

where b is the marginal propensity to consume. On the other hand, desired spending (DS) is

$$DS = C + I + G. \qquad \ldots (2)$$

Plugging (1) into (2) we get

$$DS = a + bY + I + G$$
$$= (a + I + G) + bY. \qquad \ldots (3)$$

Equation (3) gives us desired spending as a "linear" function of income with DS-intercept $(a + I + G)$ and slope b. From the figure we already know that the DS-intercept is 200. Graphically we can also see that 400 is an equilibrium level of income, where desired spending equals income. Hence, when income is 400

$$Y = DS$$
$$400 = (a + I + G) + b(400)$$
$$= 200 + b(400)$$
$$200 = b(400)$$
$$b = 0.5.$$

Therefore, the marginal propensity to consume is 0.5. Then the government spending multiplier is

$$\frac{1}{1 - MPC} = \frac{1}{1 - 0.5} = 2.$$

Since the desired increase in income is $\Delta Y = 600 - 400 = 200$, to figure out the necessary increase in government spending we compute

$$\Delta Y = \text{multiplier} \times \Delta G$$
$$200 = 2 \times \Delta G$$
$$\Delta G = 100.$$

EXAMINATION SECTION
TEST 1

DIRECTIONS: Each question or incomplete statement is followed by several suggested answers or completions. Select the one that BEST answers the question or completes the statement. *PRINT THE LETTER OF THE CORRECT ANSWER IN THE SPACE AT THE RIGHT.*

1. Of the following workers, MOST likely to be classified as structurally unemployed would be a
    A. high school teacher who is unemployed during the summer months
    B. recent college graduate who is looking for her first job
    C. teenager who is seeking part-time employment at a fast-food restaurant
    D. worker who is unemployed because his skills are obsolete
    E. woman who reenters the job market after her child begins elementary school

1.___

2. According to the classical model, an increase in the money supply causes an increase in which of the following?
    I. The price level
    II. Nominal gross national product
    III. Nominal wages

    The CORRECT answer is:
    A. I *only*   B. II *only*   C. III *only*
    D. II, III   E. I, II, III

2.___

3. If, in response to an increase in investment of $10 billion, equilibrium income rises by a total of $50 billion, then the marginal propensity to save is
    A. 0.1   B. 0.2   C. 0.5   D. 0.8   E. 0.9

3.___

4. In the circular flow diagram, which of the following is TRUE?
    A. Businesses pay wages, rent, interest, and profits to households in return for use of factors of production.
    B. Businesses purchase goods and services from households in return for money payments.
    C. Households pay wages, rent, interest, and profits to businesses in return for use of factors of production.
    D. The relationship between households and businesses exists only in a traditional society.
    E. The relationship between households and businesses exists only in a command economy.

4.___

5. Assume that the reserve requirement is 25 percent. If banks have excess reserves of $10,000, the MAXIMUM amount of additional money that can be created by the banking system through the lending process is $____.
   A. 2,500   B. 10,000   C. 40,000   D. 50,000   E. 250,000

6. According to the Keynesian model, an increase in the money supply affects output more if
   A. investment is sensitive to interest rates
   B. money demand is sensitive to interest rates
   C. the unemployment rate is low
   D. consumption is sensitive to the Phillips curve
   E. government spending is sensitive to public opinion

7. Which of the following combinations of monetary and fiscal policies is coordinated to increase output?

	Monetary Policy	Fiscal Policy
A.	Decrease the reserve requirement	Increase taxes
B.	Increase the discount rate	Increase government expenditures
C.	Sell securities	Increase taxes
D.	Sell securities	Decrease government expenditures
E.	Purchase securities	Decrease taxes

8. Which of the following is a possible cause of stagflation (simultaneous high unemployment and high inflation)?
   A. Increase in labor productivity
   B. Increase in price for raw materials
   C. The rapid growth and development of the computer industry
   D. A decline in labor union membership
   E. A low growth rate of the money supply

9. If exchange rates are allowed to fluctuate freely and the United States demand for German marks increases, which of the following will MOST likely occur?
   A. Americans will have to pay more for goods made in Germany.
   B. Germans will find that American goods are getting more expensive.
   C. The United States balance-of-payments deficit will increase.
   D. The dollar price of marks will fall.
   E. The dollar price of German goods will fall.

10. Which of the following would MOST likely be the immediate result if the United States increased tariffs on most foreign goods?
    A. The United States standard of living would be higher.
    B. More foreign goods would be purchased by Americans.
    C. Prices of domestic goods would increase.
    D. Large numbers of United States workers would be laid off.
    E. The value of the United States dollar would decrease against foreign currencies.

11. Of the following, it is TRUE that a country operating inside its production possibilities frontier
    A. has a market economy
    B. has a command economy
    C. is in the early stages of industrial development
    D. is using resources inefficiently
    E. has plentiful resources

11.___

12. Which of the following is an example of *investment* as the term is used by economists?
    A. A schoolteacher purchases 10,000 shares of stock in an automobile company.
    B. Newlyweds purchase a previously owned home.
    C. One large automobile firm purchases another large automobile firm.
    D. A farmer purchases $10,000 worth of government securities.
    E. An apparel company purchases 15 new sewing machines.

12.___

13. If the gross national product increased from $930 billion in 1969 to $975 billion in 1970 solely because of a rise in the price level, which of the following must be TRUE?
    A. Real gross national product increased between 1969 and 1970.
    B. Real gross national product decreased between 1969 and 1970.
    C. Nominal income increased between 1969 and 1970.
    D. Real income increased between 1969 and 1970.
    E. The rise in the price level between 1969 and 1970 was greater than 10 percent.

13.___

14.

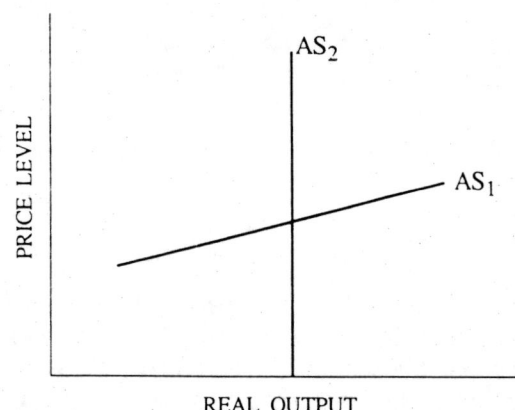

14.___

The diagram above shows two aggregate supply curves, AS_1 and AS_2.
Which of the following statements MOST accurately characterizes the AS_1 curve relative to the AS_2 curve?
AS_1 -
    A. is Keynesian because it reflects greater wage and price flexibility
    B. is classical because it reflects greater wage and price flexibility

C. is Keynesian because it reflects less wage and price flexibility
D. is classical because it reflects less wage and price flexibility
E. could be either classical or Keynesian because it reflects greater wage flexibility but less price flexibility

15. If the marginal propensity to consume is 0.9, what is the MAXIMUM amount that the equilibrium gross national product could change if government expenditures increase by $1 billion?
It could _____ by up to $_____ billion.
A. decrease; 9   B. increase; 0.9   C. increase; 1
D. increase; 9   E. increase; 10

16.
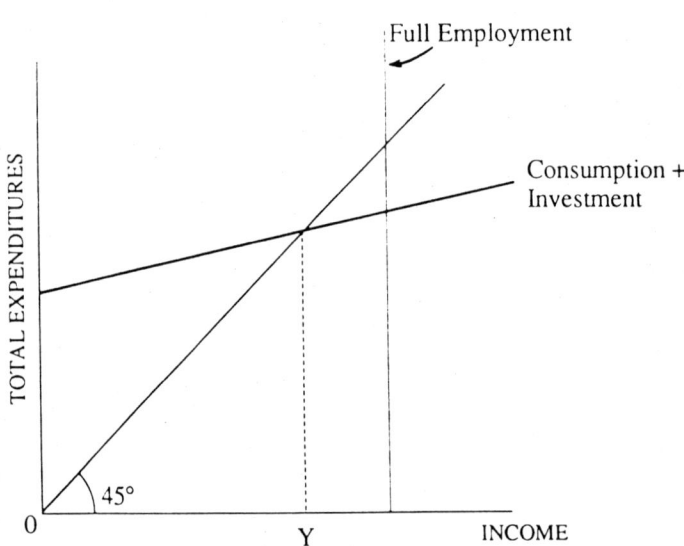

The figure above represents an economy with no government and no foreign sector.
Which of the following statements about this economy is TRUE?
At
A. Y, planned investment is less than saving
B. Y, planned investment is equal to saving
C. Y, planned investment is greater than saving
D. full employment, total spending is equal to total income
E. full employment, planned investment is equal to saving

17. According to the classical economists, which of the following is MOST sensitive to interest rates?
A. Consumption   B. Investment
C. Government spending D. Transfer payments
E. Intermediate goods

18. Expansionary fiscal policy will be MOST effective when
    A. the aggregate supply curve is horizontal
    B. the economy is at or above full-employment output
    C. transfer payments are decreased, while taxes remain unchanged
    D. wages and prices are very flexible
    E. the Federal Reserve simultaneously increases the reserve requirement

19. Which of the following would increase the value of the multiplier?
    A(n)
    A. increase in government expenditure
    B. increase in exports
    C. decrease in government unemployment benefits
    D. decrease in the marginal propensity to consume
    E. decrease in the marginal propensity to save

20. According to the monetarists, inflation is MOST often the result of
    A. high federal tax rates
    B. increased production of capital goods
    C. decreased production of capital goods
    D. an excessive growth of the money supply
    E. upward shifts in the consumption function

21. To counteract a recession, the Federal Reserve should
    A. buy securities on the open market and raise the reserve requirement
    B. buy securities on the open market and lower the reserve requirement
    C. buy securities on the open market and raise the discount rate
    D. sell securities on the open market and raise the discount rate
    E. raise the reserve requirement and lower the discount rate

22. Which of the following would result in the LARGEST increase in aggregate demand?
    A $30 billion _____ and a $30 billion _____ of government securities.
    A. increase in military expenditure; open-market purchase
    B. increase in military expenditure; open-market sale
    C. tax cut; open-market sale
    D. tax increase; open-market purchase
    E. increase in social security payments; open-market sale

23. Which of the following will be TRUE if inflation can be accurately forecast and both prices and wages are fully flexible?
    A. Long periods of high unemployment will be possible.

B. The supply of labor will be insensitive to the real wage rate.
C. The Phillips curve will be vertical.
D. The equilibrium unemployment rate will be zero.
E. Real interest rates will be greater than nominal interest rates.

24. Which of the following policies is MOST likely to encourage long-run economic growth in a country? A(n)
    A. embargo on high-technology imports
    B. decline in the number of immigrants to the country
    C. increase in government transfer payments
    D. increase in the per capita savings rate
    E. increase in defense spending

25. In one year, real gross national product fell by 3 percent, inflation rose to 10 percent, and unemployment rose to 11 percent.
    Which of the following may have caused these changes? A(n)
    A. decrease in the money supply and a decrease in government spending
    B. decrease in inflationary expectations
    C. increase in investment in inventories
    D. increase in the money supply and an increase in government spending
    E. increase in inflationary expectations

KEY (CORRECT ANSWERS)

1. D
2. E
3. B
4. A
5. C

6. A
7. E
8. B
9. A
10. C

11. D
12. E
13. C
14. C
15. E

16. B
17. B
18. A
19. E
20. D

21. B
22. A
23. C
24. D
25. E

TEST 2

DIRECTIONS: Each question or incomplete statement is followed by several suggested answers or completions. Select the one that BEST answers the question or completes the statement. *PRINT THE LETTER OF THE CORRECT ANSWER IN THE SPACE AT THE RIGHT.*

1.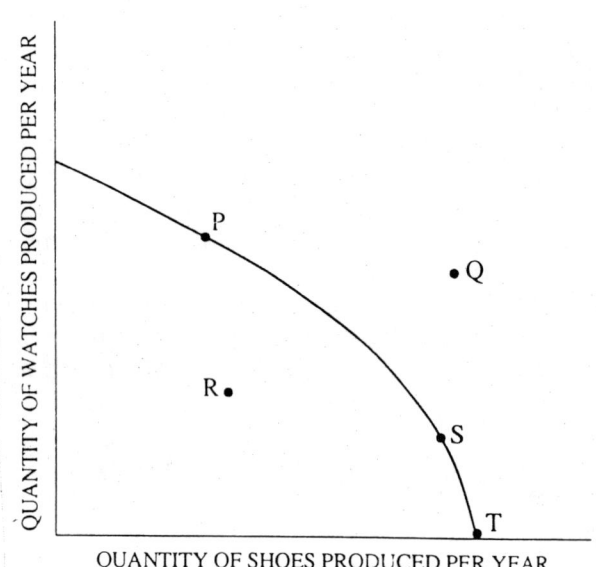

    Which of the following is TRUE of an economy with the production possibilities frontier shown above?
    A. Point Q is attainable but undesirable.
    B. Point R is unattainable but desirable.
    C. A technological improvement in the production of watches would move the economy from point T to point P.
    D. The opportunity cost of moving from point S to point T is the number of watches given up.
    E. There is unemployment at point T because workers in the watch industry are without jobs.

    1.___

2. Increases in real income per capita are made possible by
    A. improved productivity
    B. a high labor/capital ratio
    C. large trade surpluses
    D. stable interest rates
    E. high protective tariffs

    2.___

3. The sum of which of the following expenditures is equal to the value of the gross national product?
    A. Consumer purchases, investment for capital goods, exports, and imports
    B. Consumer purchases, investment for capital goods, net exports, and inventories

    3.___

4. Of the following, MOST likely to lead to a decrease in aggregate demand, that is, shift the aggregate demand curve leftward, would be a(n)
   A. decrease in taxes
   B. decrease in interest rates
   C. increase in household savings
   D. increase in household consumption
   E. increase in business firms' purchases of capital equipment from retained earnings

5. According to the Keynesian model, equilibrium output of an economy may be less than the full-employment level of output because at full employment
   A. sufficient income may not be generated to keep workers above the subsistence level
   B. there might not be enough demand by firms and consumers to buy that output
   C. workers may not be willing to work the hours necessary to produce the output
   D. interest rates might not be high enough to provide the incentive to finance the production
   E. banks may not be willing to lend enough money to support the output

6. The principal reason for requiring commercial banks to maintain reserve balances with the Federal Reserve is that these balances
   A. provide the maximum amount of reserves a bank would ever need
   B. give the Federal Reserve more control over the money-creating operations of banks
   C. ensure that banks do not make excessive profits
   D. assist the Treasury in refinancing government debt
   E. enable the government to borrow cheaply from the Federal Reserve's discount window

7. If the Federal Reserve lowers the reserve requirement, which of the following is MOST likely to happen to interest rates and gross national product?

	Interest Rates	Gross National Product
A.	Increase	Decrease
B.	Increase	Increase
C.	Decrease	Decrease
D.	Decrease	Increase
E.	No change	No change

8. Which of the following measures might be used to reduce a federal budget deficit?
   I. Raising taxes
   II. Reducing federal spending
   III. Lowering interest rates

   The CORRECT answer is:
   A. I only   B. II only   C. III only
   D. I, III   E. I, II, III

9. If the nominal interest rate is 6 percent and the expected inflation rate is 4 percent, the real interest rate is ____ percent.
   A. 10   B. 6   C. 4   D. 2   E. -2

10. Supply side economists argue that
    A. a cut in high tax rates results in an increased deficit and thus increases aggregate supply
    B. lower tax rates provide positive work incentives and thus shift the aggregate supply curve to the right
    C. the aggregate supply of goods can only be increased if the price level falls
    D. increased government spending should be used to stimulate the economy
    E. the government should regulate the supply of imports

11. If the dollar cost of the British pound decreases, United States imports from and exports to the United Kingdom will change in which of the following ways?

	Imports	Exports
A.	Increase	Decrease
B.	Increase	Increase
C.	Increase	No change
D.	Decrease	Decrease
E.	Decrease	Increase

12. An economy that is fully employing all its productive resources but allocating less to investment than to consumption will be at which of the following positions on the production possibilities curve shown at the right?
    A. A
    B. B
    C. C
    D. D
    E. E

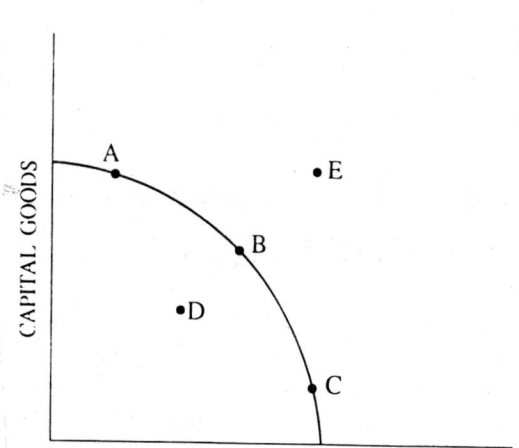

13. The United States government defines an individual as unemployed if the person
    A. does not hold a paying job
    B. has been recently fired
    C. works part-time but needs full-time work
    D. is without a job but is looking for work
    E. wants a job but is not searching because he or she thinks none is available

14. The gross national product is BEST described as a measure of
    A. economic welfare
    B. the full-employment output of an economy
    C. all monetary transactions in an economy
    D. current consumption in an economy
    E. current final output produced by an economy

15. An increase in which of the following would cause the long-run aggregate supply curve to shift to the right?
    A. Corporate income tax rates
    B. Aggregate demand
    C. Potential output
    D. The average wage rate
    E. The price level

16. Total spending in the economy is MOST likely to increase by the largest amount if which of the following occur to government spending and taxes?

	Government Spending	Taxes
A.	Decrease	Increase
B.	Decrease	No change
C.	Increase	Increase
D.	Increase	Decrease
E.	No change	Increase

17. If businesses are experiencing an unplanned increase in inventories, which of the following is MOST likely to be true?
    A. Aggregate demand is greater than output, and the level of spending will increase.
    B. Aggregate demand is less than output, and the level of spending will decrease.
    C. The economy is growing and will continue to grow until a new equilibrium level of spending is reached.
    D. Planned investment is greater than planned saving, and the level of spending will decrease.
    E. Planned investment is less than planned saving, and the level of spending will increase.

18. The purchase of securities on the open market by the Federal Reserve will
    A. increase the supply of money
    B. increase the interest rate
    C. increase the discount rate
    D. decrease the number of Federal Reserve notes in circulation
    E. decrease the reserve requirement

19. If a banking system's reserves are $100 billion, demand deposits are $500 billion, and the system is fully loaned-up, then the reserve requirement must be _____ percent.
    A. 10   B. 12.5   C. 16.6   D. 20   E. 25

20. According to the Keynesian model, an expansionary fiscal policy would tend to cause which of the following changes in output and interest rates?

	Output	Interest Rates
A.	Increase	Increase
B.	Increase	Decrease
C.	Decrease	Increase
D.	Decrease	Decrease
E.	No change	Decrease

21. Which of the following policies would MOST likely be recommended in an economy with an annual inflation rate of 3 percent and an unemployment rate of 11 percent? A(n)
    A. increase in transfer payments and an increase in the reserve requirement
    B. increase in defense spending and an increase in the discount rate
    C. increase in income tax rates and a decrease in the reserve requirement
    D. decrease in government spending and the open-market sale of government securities
    E. decrease in the tax rate on corporate profits and a decrease in the discount rate

22. The cost of reducing unemployment is accepting a higher rate of inflation.
    The statement above would MOST likely be made by a person who believes in the
    A. quantity theory of money
    B. Phillips curve
    C. theory of rational expectations
    D. paradox of value
    E. liquidity trap

23. Which of the following would occur if the international value of the United States dollar decreased?
    A. United States exports would rise.
    B. More gold would flow into the United States.
    C. United States demand for foreign currencies would increase.
    D. The United States trade deficit would increase.
    E. Americans would pay less for foreign goods.

24. Which of the following will occur as a result of an improvement in technology?
    The _____ curve will shift _____.
    A. aggregate demand; to the right
    B. aggregate demand; to the left
    C. aggregate supply; to the right
    D. aggregate supply; to the left
    E. production possibilities; inward

25. Assume that land in an agricultural economy can be used either for producing grain or for grazing cattle to produce beef.
The opportunity cost of converting an acre from cattle grazing to grain production is the
   A. market value of the extra grain that is produced
   B. total amount of beef produced
   C. number of extra bushels of grain that are produced
   D. amount by which beef production decreases
   E. profits generated by the extra production of grain

25.___

KEY (CORRECT ANSWERS)

1. D	11. A
2. A	12. C
3. C	13. D
4. C	14. E
5. B	15. C
6. B	16. D
7. D	17. B
8. E	18. A
9. D	19. D
10. B	20. A

21. E
22. B
23. A
24. C
25. D

EXAMINATION SECTION

DIRECTIONS: Each question or incomplete statement is followed by several suggested answers or completions. Select the one that BEST answers the question or completes the statement. *PRINT THE LETTER OF THE CORRECT ANSWER IN THE SPACE AT THE RIGHT.*

1. What is the present value of $121 to be received one year from now if the rate of interest is 10 percent each year?
    A. $12.10   B. $100.00   C. $110.00
    D. $121.00   E. $133.10

1.___

Questions 2-3.

DIRECTIONS: Questions 2 and 3 are to be answered on the basis of the table below, which represents the joint probabilities of a consumer purchasing two products, X and Y.

	Purchases Y	Does Not Purchase Y
Purchases X	.10	.30
Does Not Purchase X	.40	.20

(e.g., *.30* means that the probability is .3 that a randomly chosen consumer purchases X <u>and</u> does not purchase Y)

2. Given that a consumer purchases Y, what is the probability that the consumer will also purchase X?
    A. .20   B. .25   C. .30   D. .40   E. .50

2.___

3. If X costs $1 per unit and Y costs $2 per unit, what is the expected amount of money spent on the two products by a randomly chosen consumer?
    A. $0.80   B. $1.00   C. $1.10   D. $1.40   E. $2.00

3.___

4. Compared with a large closed economy, a small open economy with a fixed exchange rate will have a _____ domestic multiplier _____ control over the domestic money stock.
    A. smaller; and less   B. smaller; and more
    C. larger; and less   D. larger; and more
    E. larger; but the same

4.___

5. The imposition of an import tariff will result in which of the following?
   I. A reduction in the volume of world trade
   II. A reduction in the gains from world trade
   III. A distortion in the allocation of resources from that indicated by comparative advantage

   The CORRECT answer is:
   A. I only B. II only C. I, II
   D. II, III E. I, II, III

6.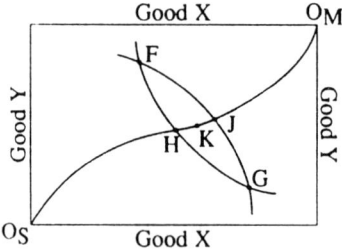

   In the above diagram, $O_M O_S$ is the contract curve. Among the points specifically labeled in the diagram, a Pareto-optimal distribution of goods X and Y between consumers S and M can occur at
   A. F only B. K only C. F or G
   D. H or J E. H or J or K

Questions 7-8.

DIRECTIONS: Questions 7 and 8 are to be answered on the basis of the following simple (two-variable) regression model.

where $Y_i = a + bX_i + c_i$

   Y = dependent variable
   X = independent variable
   c = disturbance (or error) term
   a,b are parameters
   subscript i refers to the ith observation

7. Which of the following is usually assumed in this model? The
   A. expected value of the disturbance term, e, is zero
   B. variance of the disturbance term is unity
   C. variance of the independent variable, X, is unity
   D. dependent variable, Y, is uncorrelated with the disturbance term, e
   E. covariance of the independent variable, X, and the disturbance term, e, is unity

8. If, in addition to the relationship postulated above, the independent variable, X, is a linear function of Y, then which of the following will be TRUE?
   A. Autocorrelation will exist among the disturbance terms.
   B. The disturbance terms will be heteroscedastic.
   C. The ordinary least-squares estimators of a and b will be biased.
   D. The estimated standard errors will tend to be quite large because of multi-collinearity.
   E. A dummy variable will be needed to control for this additional relationship.

9. Externalities tend to introduce misallocations of resources into a competitive market system because
   A. individual producers no longer maximize profits
   B. market prices do not accurately reflect true social costs and benefits
   C. balance-of-payments deficits and surpluses generally result
   D. externalities typically result in a more unequal distribution of income
   E. externalities cause unemployment

10. Which of the following policy changes represents an unambiguously contractionary monetary policy?

	Open-Market Operations	Reserve Requirements	Discount Rate
A.	Sale of securities	Increase	Increase
B.	Sale of securities	Increase	Decrease
C.	Purchase of securities	Increase	Increase
D.	Purchase of securities	Decrease	Increase
E.	Purchase of securities	Decrease	Decrease

11. Which of the following would be MOST likely to induce a monopolist to set an output and a price approaching those that would prevail in a competitive market?
    A. A tax on the monopolist's output
    B. A tax on the monopolist's profits
    C. A subsidy on the monopolist's output
    D. A prescribed minimum selling price for the monopolist's product
    E. Advertising of the monopolist's product

12. It has been estimated that the income elasticity of demand for cars is approximately 1.8.
    This figure should be interpreted to mean that if income increases by _____ the demand for cars will increase by _____.
    A. 10%; 1.8% B. 10%; 18% C. 18%; 10%
    D. $100; $180 E. $180; $100

13. If the level of nominal net national product is rising during a period in which the money supply is constant, which of the following must also be TRUE?
    A. Prices must be rising.
    B. Prices must be constant.
    C. The velocity of money must be rising.
    D. The velocity of money must be constant.
    E. Real net national product must be rising.

Questions 14-15.

DIRECTIONS: Questions 14 and 15 are to be answered on the basis of the following IS-LM diagram.

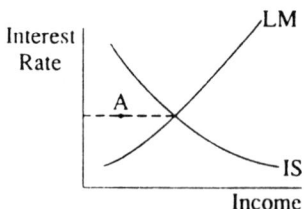

14. At the income-interest rate combination given by point A, there is an excess
    A. supply of goods and an excess supply of money
    B. supply of goods and an excess demand for money
    C. demand for goods, but the money market is in equilibrium
    D. demand for goods and an excess demand for money
    E. demand for goods and an excess supply of money

15. Other things remaining the same, an increase in tax rates causes the equilibrium level of income to
    A. fall and the interest rate to fall
    B. fall and the interest rate to rise
    C. fall, and leaves the equilibrium level of the interest rate unchanged
    D. rise and the interest rate to rise
    E. rise and the interest rate to fall

16. If average total cost increases as output increases, which of the following must be TRUE?
    A. Marginal cost must be constant.
    B. Average fixed cost must be increasing.
    C. Fixed cost must be increasing.
    D. Average variable cost must be greater than average fixed cost.
    E. Marginal cost must be greater than average total cost.

17. If a consumer of two goods possesses indifference curves that have everywhere a constant marginal rate of substitution, the consumer's utility-maximizing purchases will MOST likely include
    A. equal expenditures on both goods
    B. equal amounts of both goods
    C. some of both goods, but in unequal amounts
    D. one good only
    E. unspent income

18. According to the *factor-proportions* argument, urban unemployment may rise during the process of economic development because urban and rural areas use factors in
    A. different proportions and elasticities of substitution are high
    B. different proportions and elasticities of substitution are low
    C. the same proportions and elasticities of substitution are high
    D. the same proportions and elasticities of substitution are low
    E. the same proportions regardless of the elasticities of substitution

19. Which of the following would be a coordinated combination of fiscal and monetary policies instituted to decrease aggregate demand?

	Fiscal Policy	Monetary Policy
A.	Decrease in government expenditures	Decrease in reserve requirement
B.	Increase in government expenditures	Increase in reserve requirement
C.	Decrease in personal income tax rates	Central-bank sale of government securities in the open market
D.	Increase in personal income tax rates	Central-bank purchase of government securities in the open market
E.	Increase in personal income tax rates	Central-bank sale of government securities in the open market

Questions 20-21.

DIRECTIONS: Questions 20 and 21 are to be answered on the basis of the following demand and cost functions for a good.

$P = 20 - 0.5Q$
$C = 75 + 5Q$

where
P = price
Q = quantity
C = total cost

20. The level of output of a profit-maximizing monopolist would be
    A. 5   B. 10   C. 15   D. 20   E. 30

21. If the rest of the economy is perfectly competitive, the level of output that would achieve optimal use of resources would be
    A. 5   B. 10   C. 15   D. 20   E. 30

22. Which of the following did NOT contribute to the eighteenth-century Industrial Revolution in Britain?
    A. Rapid technological change in the textile industry
    B. Enclosure and consolidation of agricultural lands
    C. Introduction of gold as a convenient medium of exchange
    D. Increased trade with other nations
    E. Invention and application of the steam engine

23. Assume that the population is growing at 2 percent per year and that the capital output ratio is 4 to 1. Approximately what percent of gross national product must be saved and invested if per capita output is to rise by 1 percent per year?
    A. 6%   B. 8%   C. 9%   D. 12%   E. 16%

Questions 24-25.

DIRECTIONS: Questions 24 and 25 are to be answered on the basis of the following Cobb-Douglas production function.

$$Q = AK^a L^{1-a}$$

where
  Q = output
  K = capital
  L = labor
  A = a constant, where $A > 0$
  a = a constant, where $0 < a < 1$

24. In this production function, the marginal product of labor is equal to
    A. K/L
    B. $(1-a)$
    C. A
    D. $a(Q/K)$
    E. $(1-a)(Q/L)$

25. Which of the following statements concerning this production function is FALSE?
    A. The production function is homogeneous of degree one.
    B. For given prices of K and L, the long-run average cost curve is U-shaped.
    C. For a given K, the marginal physical product of L will decrease when L is increased.
    D. At given prices for K and L, factor proportions are independent of the level of output.
    E. If the firm is a perfect competitor in factor and final product markets, its equilibrium size is indeterminate.

26. Two countries, T and Z, produce only two goods, cloth and meat, using labor as the only input. Each country has 100 workers. The production processes in both countries are subject to constant returns to scale. The table below shows the maximum daily output of each commodity in each country if all of that country's labor is allocated to industry.

Country	Cloth(yards)	Meat(pounds)
T	10	30
Z	20	40

Which of the following statements is(are) correct?
   I. Z has a comparative advantage in meat.
   II. Z has a comparative advantage in cloth.
   III. Z has an absolute advantage in both goods.

The CORRECT answer is:
   A. I *only*   B. II *only*   C. III *only*
   D. I, II   E. II, III

Questions 27-28.

DIRECTIONS: Questions 27 and 28 are to be answered on the basis of the following macromodel of a closed economy. All data are in billions of dollars.

$$Y = C + I + G$$
$$C = .8(Y-T)$$
$$I = 40 + .1Y$$

where
   Y = income
   C = consumption
   I = investment
   G = government expenditures
   T = taxes

27. If there are no taxes or government expenditures, what is the equilibrium level of national income? _____ billion.
   A. $60   B. $100   C. $400   D. $500   E. $800

28. Now assume the government levies an income tax of 25 percent and simultaneously undertakes expenditures in an amount that balances the budget.
What is the equilibrium level of national income? _____ billion.
   A. $200   B. $400   C. $600   D. $800   E. $1,200

29. An entrepreneur reports, *I'm losing money but I am not shutting down.*
Given that the entrepreneur's firm is attempting to maximize profits in the short run, this reaction is
   A. rational if the firm is covering its variable costs
   B. rational if the firm is covering its fixed costs
   C. rational if the firm's expectations are rational
   D. irrational since the firm will not have to incur fixed costs when the plant is shut down
   E. irrational since closing the plant is necessary to eliminate losses

30. In a typical set of national income and product accounts in the absence of a government sector, the sum of factor incomes equals the value of total output because
   A. factor shares sum to unity with a Cobb-Douglas production function
   B. net worth is a balance-sheet residual that ensures equality
   C. profits are a residual equal to the value of output minus payments to other factors
   D. investment is equal to savings plus depreciation
   E. expenditures by consumers are equal to wage payments to workers

31. A person sells $100,000 in government bonds to the central bank.
If the person puts the cash proceeds in a safe-deposit box, then the money supply (M1) will
   A. be unchanged and the supply of bank reserves will also remain the same
   B. be unchanged but the supply of bank reserves will increase by $100,000
   C. increase by $100,000
   D. increase by some multiple of $100,000 that will depend on the legal reserve ratio
   E. decrease by $100,000 because the proceeds have been removed from circulation

KEY (CORRECT ANSWERS)

1. C	11. C	21. E
2. A	12. B	22. C
3. D	13. C	23. D
4. A	14. E	24. E
5. E	15. A	25. B
6. E	16. E	26. E
7. A	17. D	27. C
8. C	18. B	28. D
9. B	19. E	29. A
10. A	20. C	30. C
		31. C

EXAMINATION SECTION

DIRECTIONS: Each question or incomplete statement is followed by several suggested answers or completions. Select the one that BEST answers the question or completes the statement. *PRINT THE LETTER OF THE CORRECT ANSWER IN THE SPACE AT THE RIGHT.*

1. WHICH of the following are examples of leakage from the circular flow of money?
   I. Personal savings
   II. Business savings
   III. Government expenditures
   IV. Exports
   V. Tax collections
   The CORRECT answer is:
   A. I, IV
   B. I, II, V
   C. I, IV, V
   D. III, IV, V
   E. III, IV

1.____

2. WHAT is the MAIN difference between "token coins" and "full-bodied money"? They
   A. are metal
   B. are less valuable
   C. are marked with a sign of authority
   D. bear a distinguishing mark
   E. show no difference

2.____

3. The BULK of money in the United States is in the form of
   A. coins and paper money
   B. time deposits
   C. demand deposits
   D. cash value of insurance policies
   E. savings and loan association shares

3.____

4. HOW do commercial banks differ from other financial institutions? They can
   A. handle time deposits
   B. invest in government securities
   C. channel the savings of households into private investment
   D. issue currency
   E. create money

4.____

5. WHAT is (are) the component(s) of currency?
   I. Federal Reserve notes
   II. Coins
   III. Silver dollars
   IV. Silver certificates
   V. U.S. notes
   The CORRECT answer is:
   A. I *only*
   B. II, III
   C. I, IV, V
   D. I, II, III, V
   E. All of the above

5.____

6. The Keynesian "liquidity trap" defines a situation wherein
   A. suppliers of money compete in the market for loanable funds
   B. disposable money is kept from responding to changes in the GNP
   C. firms and households do not invest excessive money

6.____

D. investors are induced to borrow more money in order to invest more
E. the interest elasticity of investment and consumption is small

7. WHAT the consuming sector of the economy spends is called 7.___
   A. consumption   B. net investment
   C. expenditures   D. disposable income
   E. net transfers

8. WHICH economy is the BEST example of hyperinflation? 8.___
   A. Germany following World War I
   B. Russia following the 1917 Revolution
   C. Great Britain following World War II
   D. the United States following the Korean War
   E. the United States following the Vietnam War

9. WHAT are the "dependent" variables of macroeconomic theory? 9.___
   I. The rate of change in the general price level
   II. Changes in the production function
   III. Changes in unemployment
   IV. Changes in the aggregate supply function
   V. Changes in population
   The CORRECT answer is:
   A. I, II, IV   B. I, III   C. II, IV, V
   D. I, III, V   E. II, IV

10. WHAT causes structural-demand inflation? When 10.___
    A. the purchasing power of money and government bonds in the hands of the private sector increases
    B. prices in industries with weak demand do not decline
    C. prices rise even though producers cannot meet demand
    D. entrepreneurs increase investment
    E. the government boosts aggregate demand

11. WHAT is the basic principle of the stabilization policy of the "Swedish budget"? That 11.___
    A. government expenditures should be solely determined by public needs
    B. an index of economic activity should be designed
    C. consumption is a stable function
    D. technological innovation is external to the economic system
    E. interest rates should not be manipulated

12. HOW does the stabilization theory of "formula flexibility" attempt to stabilize the economy? By 12.___
    A. discretionary tax reductions or increases in government expenditures
    B. having the central bank dominate the level of the monetary base
    C. having tax rates automatically respond to changes in economic activity
    D. manipulating the stock of money
    E. having money accelerate and decelerate according to economic cycles

13. WHAT are the drawbacks to the gold-flow mechanism to correct trade imbalances? It
    I. results in nations exporting unemployment problems to others
    II. relies on inflation and deflation
    III. relies on price levels that may not respond quickly enough to gold movements
    IV. relies on currency valuation changes
    V. relies on speculative movements of capital
    The CORRECT answer is:
    A. I, IV B. I, V C. I, IV, V
    D. II, III E. IV, V

14. WHICH of the following give rise to the purchase of foreign currency?
    I. Capital imports
    II. Foreign aid
    III. Tourism in the United States
    IV. News that the government intends to devalue the currency
    V. U.S. military personnel stationed in foreign countries
    The CORRECT answer is:
    A. I, V B. III, IV C. I, II, IV
    D. II, III, IV E. I, IV, V

15. WHAT is "hot money"?
    A. Capital used for speculation prior to and after a devaluation of currency
    B. Capital used to purchase future foreign currencies
    C. The external price of currency
    D. Currency loaned by the International Monetary Fund
    E. Undesirable currency

16. WHAT is the ONLY REAL SERVICE rendered by gold in a modern economy? It
    A. *facilitates* foreign trade
    B. *determines* the supply of money
    C. *gives* currency value
    D. *deters* economic cycles
    E. *produces* a value that is constant

17. WHAT is the speciality of mutual savings banks?
    A. Investments in government securities
    B. Checking accounts
    C. Investments in residential construction
    D. Long-term loans
    E. Investments in real estate

18. WHICH of the following motives for holding money is(are) NEGATIVELY related to the interest rate? The _____ motive.
    A. precautionary motive and the speculative
    B. speculative
    C. transactions motive and the speculative
    D. transactions motive and the precautionary
    E. transactions

19. The CHIEF item separating net national product from disposable income is
    A. depreciation
    B. retained earnings
    C. transfer payments
    D. expenditures
    E. net taxes

20. HOW does the government increase the high-powered money in the economy? By
    A. printing money
    B. selling bonds to the central bank
    C. changing government spending and the level of taxes
    D. selling securities to the private sector
    E. generating optimism in the business and financial communities

21. WHAT is the central variation in macroeconomic theory that explains changes in unemployment and inflation? Variation in the
    A. production function
    B. aggregate-supply function
    C. efficiency-change function
    D. growth rate of real output
    E. labor force participation function

22. WHAT is the GREATEST impediment to a smoothly functioning stabilization policy in the United States?
    A. The increase of union strength within the economy
    B. Continued growth of the public debt
    C. Social considerations
    D. Timing the implementation of stabilizing tools
    E. Lack of knowledge of factors affecting investment

23. WHAT is the basic principle of the stabilization policy of "formula flexibility"?
    A. That for each debtor there is a creditor
    B. To promote maximum employment
    C. To determine the velocity of circulation
    D. Delegating limited powers of changing tax rates to the Executive Branch
    E. To design an index of economic activity

24. WHAT is the MAIN advantage of the stabilization policy of "formula flexibility"? It
    A. smoothes the ups and downs of economic activity
    B. provides actual measurement of the macroeconomic variables
    C. provides a formula that separates the rise in price from the rise in quality
    D. provides a method of estimating the potential GNP
    E. is divorced from political arbitrariness

25. WHICH of the following describes devaluation without depreciation? It is a
    A. situation wherein price changes increase exports
    B. situation wherein the value of one country's currency declines relative to another country's

C. process of changing price levels until a relative price level occurs
D. situation that leads to higher levels of domestic production at the expense of foreign goods
E. process akin to printing high-powered money

26. WHICH of the following factors RAISE the price of foreign currency?
   I. Economic expansion and boom within the United States
   II. A change in the tastes of foreign consumers in favor of American commodities
   III. A change in the tastes of foreign entrepreneurs in favor of investing in the United States
   IV. Technological changes within the United States
   V. Increased investment abroad
   The CORRECT answer is:
   A. I, II, III   B. III, IV, V   C. II, III
   D. II, III, IV   E. I, V

27. WHAT meaning does "hedging" have in international trade? It means
   A. purchasers refuse to commit themselves in advance to a purchase
   B. purchasing future foreign currency at a predetermined rate of exchange
   C. sellers will only accept hard currency for purchases
   D. purchasers fixing the price of an item at the time the order is placed
   E. methods used to guard against increased outflows of capital

28. WHY should a government HESITATE to counter depressionary tendencies by devaluating its currency? It
   A. changes price levels
   B. decreases exports
   C. adversely affects international harmony and goodwill
   D. cures one problem at the expense of the entire economy
   E. causes nations to retaliate by imposing strict controls on movements of commodities and capital

29. The monetarist or traditional approach to stabilization emphasizes the role played by the
   A. Council of Economic Advisors
   B. Congress
   C. Federal Reserve Board
   D. public and commercial banking system
   E. Joint Economic Committee of Congress

30. A growing public debt
   A. is evidence of government mismanagement
   B. is a burden for future generations
   C. impedes a smoothly functioning stabilization policy
   D. does not cause instability or interfere with policies to stabilize the economy
   E. inhibits the economy's long-run tendency to expand

31. WHICH of the following are TRUE of the American economy?
     I. Stable total demand is never produced by the American system
    II. Short-run fluctuations of total demand are influenced by changes in business investment expenditures
   III. The mechanism setting boundaries to short-run fluctuations are inherent in the system
    IV. Changes in interest rates are largely explained by changes in the rate of increase of the money supply
     V. The market economy is generally capable of self-feeding change in total demand in either direction without limit
    The CORRECT answer is:
    A. I, III, IV   B. I, II, V   C. II, III, IV
    D. II, V   E. I, II, IV

32. Macroeconomic theory is the theory of all of the following EXCEPT
    A. prices
    B. money
    C. production and consumption
    D. employment
    E. income

33. During a "repressed inflation," inflationary pressures are repressed by
    A. limited excess reserves of commercial banks
    B. forced saving
    C. the amount of money held for transaction purposes
    D. a low rate of interest
    E. a lack of high-powered money in the economy

34. The "Pigou Effect" is based on the fact that
    A. for each debtor there is a creditor
    B. supply creates its own demand
    C. investment is proportional to changes in output
    D. desired capital is a function of the level of output
    E. government debt is held by financial institutions and firms all over the country

35. WHAT is the ESSENTIAL role of the central bank? To
    A. *create* money
    B. *regulate* the amount of currency in circulation
    C. *establish* interest rates
    D. *regulate* the supply of money in the economy
    E. *align* prices with money supplies

36. The "stock of money" is the sum of
     I. currency in circulation
    II. demand deposits in commercial banks
   III. U.S. bonds
    IV. time deposits
     V. certificates of deposit
    The CORRECT answer is:
    A. I, II   B. I, III   C. I, IV
    D. I, II, IV   E. All of the above

37. According to the classical economists, *WHAT* brings the market for funds into equilibrium? The
    A. interest rate
    B. quantity of money supplied by savers
    C. composition of the market for funds
    D. number of investors
    E. difference between the number of investors and the number of savers

38. The proportion of consumption to disposable personal income
    A. decreases with the growth of income per capita over time
    B. has changed significantly since the Great Depression
    C. increases even with a decline of income per capita over time
    D. does not diminish over time in spite of the growth of income per capita over time
    E. is dependent upon the GNP

39. *WHICH* of the following is (are) unconditionally legal tender?
    I. Time deposits   II. Demand deposits
  III. U.S. bonds   IV. Coins
    V. Paper money
 The *CORRECT* answer is:
    A. I, II, IV, V   B. III, IV, V   C. IV *only*
    D. V *only*   E. None of the above

40. *WHAT* is the speciality of savings and loan associations?
    A. Transferring savings to investment in real estate
    B. Time deposits
    C. Long-term loans
    D. Investment in private business
    E. Demand deposits

41. *WHAT* is the "public debt"? The unpaid amount
    A. the public has borrowed
    B. business firms have borrowed
    C. the federal government has borrowed
    D. commercial banks have borrowed
    E. the public and business firms have borrowed

42. *WHEN* is an economic stabilizer considered to be "built-in" to the system? When
    A. laws exist to govern phases of the cycle
    B. it begins to operate automatically over the cycle
    C. it promotes maximum employment
    D. it is easily set in motion
    E. it is impervious to economic changes

43. *WHAT* explains the response of output and price level to any given growth rate of total demand? The theory of
    A. real output   B. production
    C. economic development   D. total demand
    E. the aggregate-supply function

44. WHICH of the following are true when American exports fall short of American imports? It leads to
   I. a reduction in gold reserves of the Federal Reserve System
   II. a reduction in the foreign currency reserves of the Federal Reserve System
   III. an increase in the purchase of foreign currency
   IV. a decrease in the purchase of foreign currency
   V. the imposition of administrative controls on exports
   The CORRECT answer is:
   A. I, II, III
   B. I, II, IV
   C. II, V
   D. I, IV, V
   E. I, II, V

45. WHAT is an objection to a flexible exchange rate? It
   A. can cause governments to impose administrative restrictions on trade
   B. interferes with the price of currency being determined in the free market
   C. causes the central bank to synchronize the inflow and outflow of foreign currencies
   D. gives rise to inflationary pressures
   E. could lead to a reduced level of world trade

46. Macroeconomic theory and practice is largely influenced by
   A. international trade
   B. political implications
   C. differences between economists
   D. public opinion
   E. available information

47. WHICH of the following is (are) the preferred method of the Federal Reserve System for changing the economy's supply of money?
   A. Open market operations
   B. Discounting policies
   C. Changing the reserve ratio
   D. Discounting policies and changing the reserve ratio
   E. Open market operations and discounting policies

48. Currency consists PRIMARILY of
   A. coins
   B. silver dollars
   C. silver certificates
   D. U.S. notes
   E. Federal Reserve notes

49. WHAT was the MAIN disadvantage of the gold standard?
   A. The supply of money was limited by legislation
   B. The supply of money was not determined by the needs of the economy
   C. Changing gold supplies caused inflations and recessions
   D. It limited the supply of money
   E. Prices were unable to adjust to fluctuations in gold production

50. The ratio of Disposable Personal Income to Gross National   50.____
    Product is determined to a very large extent by
    A. financial institutions
    B. the government
    C. the flexibility of prices
    D. consumers
    E. the net export of goods and services

KEY (CORRECT ANSWERS)

1. B	11. A	21. D	31. B	41. C
2. B	12. C	22. D	32. C	42. B
3. C	13. D	23. E	33. B	43. E
4. E	14. C	24. E	34. A	44. B
5. E	15. A	25. B	35. D	45. E
6. C	16. A	26. E	36. A	46. B
7. A	17. D	27. B	37. A	47. E
8. A	18. A	28. C	38. D	48. E
9. B	19. E	29. C	39. D	49. B
10. B	20. B	30. D	40. A	50. B

EXAMINATION SECTION

DIRECTIONS: Each question or incomplete statement is followed by several suggested answers or completions. Select the one that BEST answers the question or completes the statement. *PRINT THE LETTER OF THE CORRECT ANSWER IN THE SPACE AT THE RIGHT.*

1. World trade is *NOT* based *SOLELY* on gold because 1.____
   A. gold is too costly
   B. the value of gold is not fixed
   C. the value of gold fluctuates with market conditions
   D. gold is not liquid enough
   E. the world's supply of gold is limited

2. How was adjustment of international trade achieved under the gold standard? Through 2.____
   A. changes in currency valuation
   B. administrative controls
   C. changes in price levels
   D. a balance of payments
   E. exchange rates

3. The fiscal policy used to fight against inflation is *MOST LIKELY* to be one that 3.____
   A. reduces government expenditures
   B. raises interest rates
   C. raises personal or corporate tax rates
   D. lowers the required reserve ratio
   E. increases government expenditures

4. Gross National Product is a measure of 4.____
   A. the net creation of new wealth resulting from the productive activity of the economy
   B. the market value of goods and services sold during the year
   C. prices
   D. production
   E. investment expenditures

5. *WHAT* is Knut Wicksell's *MAIN* objection to the classical economists' view of market equilibrium? 5.____
   A. Supply does not create its own demand
   B. Savers cannot be induced to postpone consumption by raising interest rates
   C. Financial institutions are not fully responsive to market conditions
   D. Equilibrium cannot be achieved with a net leakage
   E. The result of market equilibrium is deflation

6. Metals were used as a medium of exchange for all the following reasons *EXCEPT* it 6.____
   A. is abundant   B. can be stored   C. is divisible
   D. is homogeneous   E. is valued for its beauty

7. WHAT is meant by the phrase, "Full Employment"? 7. ____
   A. The difference between the number of jobs available and the number of workers unemployed
   B. A zero unemployment rate
   C. The difference between the number of jobs available and the number of people who are out of the labor force
   D. Jobs for all people in the labor force
   E. The difference between the number of persons unemployed and the number of unfilled jobs

8. WHICH of the following is TRUE? 8. ____
   A. The poor consume more than the rich
   B. The rich consume a larger proportion of their income than the poor
   C. The poor save a larger proportion of their income than the rich
   D. Consumption is a stable function of disposable personal income
   E. The rich and poor consume a nearly identical proportion of their incomes

9. WHAT is the MAIN difference between "money" and "near-money"? 9. ____
   A. Value   B. Acceptability   C. Convenience
   D. Amount   E. Liability

10. HOW does the Federal Reserve System increase the money supply? By 10. ____
    I. buying government bonds from the commercial banks
    II. selling government securities to the private sector
    III. lowering the rediscount rate of the central government
    IV. reducing the required reserve ratio of commercial banks
    V. increasing membership in the Federal Reserve System
    The CORRECT answer is:
    A. I, V   B. I, III, IV   C. II, III, IV
    D. II, IV   E. II, IV, V

11. WHY is a tax-cut during a recession more desirable than raising government expenditures. It 11. ____
    A. helps alleviate some of the poverty in the private sector
    B. allows private citizens the choice of how to spend additional expenditures
    C. achieves full employment faster
    D. is a more straightfoward policy
    E. allows the government to sell securities to private persons

12. Inflation FAVORS 12. ____
    A. creditors   B. employers
    C. pension recipients   D. insurance recipients
    E. borrowers

13. WHICH of the following are TRUE of a tight-money   13.____
    policy? It
        I. leads to higher interest rates
       II. is aimed at shrinking the aggregate demand for
           final goods and services
      III. affects all industries
       IV. is a remedy for an economy moving toward recession
        V. is achieved by boosting the discount rate
    The CORRECT answer is:
        A. I, II   B. II, III   C. I, II, V
        D. III, IV   E. III, IV, V

14. WHAT is the MAIN objection to the stabilization policy   14.____
    which prevails in the United States? It
        A. does not guarantee full employment
        B. attempts to force the economy into a perennial
           recession
        C. is entirely a function of the Executive Department
        D. depends on Congress's responding to the needs for
           ad hoc fiscal changes
        E. overreacts to the economic cycles

15. Macroeconomic aspects of international trade arise   15.____
    because
        A. countries engage in commerce
        B. countries have different currencies
        C. not all countries are on the gold standard
        D. trade imbalances cause economic instability
        E. unemployment can be exported

16. When an American purchases foreign securities, it is   16.____
    called
        A. short-term credit   B. long-term credit
        C. a capital export   D. a capital import
        D. a long-term debit

17. The volume of international trade is ENHANCED by   17.____
        A. barter arrangements
        B. use of gold for payment
        C. use of an international currency for payment
        D. use of currency acceptable to all for payment
        E. use of legal tender for all payments

18. When the gold standard was in effect, countries achieved 18.____
    a balance of trade through
        A. a foreign trade multiplier
        B. hedging
        C. short-term credits
        D. the rate of exchange
        E. the gold-flow mechanism

19. WHICH of the following are considered triggering   19.____
    mechanisms for less than full-employment inflation? When
        I. powerful trade unions force employers to pay wage increases
       II. firms raise prices because of agreements with each
           other not to engage in price competition

III. prices in weak industries do not decline as those in high-demand industries rise
IV. a boom occurs in the business world
V. the government imposes forced-saving controls on the economy

The CORRECT answer is:
A. I, II, III   B. II, IV   C. I, V
D. II, III   E. I, II, V

20. The sum of retained earnings and depreciation of business is called
 A. Transfer Payments
 B. Net Investment
 C. Gross Business Savings
 D. Net Savings
 E. Disposable Income

21. WHICH of the following specialize in time deposits?
 I. Savings and Loan Associations
 II. Mutual Savings Banks
 III. Life Insurance Companies
 IV. Commercial Banks
 V. Commodity Banks

The CORRECT answer is:
A. I, II   B. I, II, III   C. II, IV
D. IV, V   E. III, IV, V

22. All of the following are TRUE of inflation EXCEPT:
 A. Inflation is relative from a time and geographic perspective
 B. Inflation may occur during booms
 C. Seasonal changes in price levels cannot be described as inflationary
 D. Inflation is caused by rising prices
 E. Inflationary situations are usually open to interpretation

23. WHICH of the following are TRUE of the transactions motive for holding money?
 I. It is not without cost
 II. Both households and firms hold only the bare minimum amount which is needed
 III. Households are motivated to hold money because of unforeseen emergencies
 IV. The higher the interest rate, the smaller the demand for holding money
 V. Firms hold money because receiving revenue does not coincide in time with payments

The CORRECT answer is:
A. I, IV   B. I, III, V   C. I, II, V
D. I, IV, V   E. I, III, IV

24. Macroeconomic Theory reflects a certain social   24.____
    philosophy because it is concerned with
    A. the prevention of large-scale unemployment
    B. economic loss
    C. the causes and effects of inflation
    D. the determination and significance of interest rates
    E. the theory of income for individual households

25. *HOW* does the "Swedish budget" achieve stabilization?   25.____
    By
    A. lowering the tax rates during recessions and
       raising the tax rates during booms
    B. providing that government stockpiles of materials
       should be purchased in periods of weak demand and
       then drawn upon when demand becomes very tight
    C. lowering the required reserve ratio during re-
       cessions and raising it during inflationary periods
    D. increasing government expenditures during recessions
       and cutting back expenditures during inflations
    E. maintaining policies which will keep the changing
       levels of investment from severely disturbing the
       economy

26. *WHAT* is the MAIN difference between a pegged exchange   26.____
    rate and a flexible exchange rate? The MAIN difference
    lies in how
    A. the exchange rate is determined
    B. credit is extended
    C. gold is exchanged
    D. adjustment to market conditions is achieved
    E. the external price of currency is measured

27. *WHAT* is the role of the International Monetary Fund?   27.____
    To
    A. extend credit
    B. fix exchange rates
    C. impose controls on movements of commodities
       and capital
    D. facilitate international trade
    E. prevent another worldwide depression

28. *WHICH* factor affects the level of investment the MOST?   28.____
    A. Rate of interest
    B. Expectations of entrepreneurs
    C. Technological innovations
    D. Taxation
    E. Wage rate

29. When a business boom causes an inflation, it is *LIMITED*   29.____
    by the
    A. gap between excess demand over supply
    B. interest rate
    C. limited creation of high-powered money
    D. tax increases
    E. velocity of money

30. The commercial banking system is NEVER fully loaned-up because
    A. of legal reserve requirements
    B. money leaks out of the system
    C. money cannot be created
    D. of the amount of currency held by the public
    E. there are too many separate banks

31. WHICH of the following are TRUE of money? Money is
    I. necessary to continue to produce and exchange real commodities
    II. necessary to produce and consume as much as we currently do
    III. necessary for the functioning of a modern economy
    IV. essential to the process of exchange in a modern economy
    V. the only commodity that serves as a store of value
    The CORRECT answer is:
    A. I, III, V   B. I, II, III, IV   C. III, V
    D. II, III, IV   E. All of the above

32. WHAT causes the supply of money to change in a commercial banking system? The
    A. excess reserve situation
    B. amount of currency in circulation
    C. amount of currency held by the public
    D. number of banking branches
    E. number of loans issued

33. The Keynesian "liquidity trap" is LEAST LIKELY to occur when
    A. the Federal Reserve System publicizes use of the discount rate tool
    B. a monetary policy is not applied at the outset of the recession
    C. the recession is severe
    D. the recession is mild
    E. firms expect prices to continue to fall

34. WHICH of the following are TRUE of hyperinflation? It
    I. is characterized by a mild but steady rise in the general price level
    II. occurs when the government creates far too much money
    III. causes households and firms to hold too much money
    IV. causes the purchasing power of money to decline
    V. decreases the velocity of money
    The CORRECT answer is :
    A. I, II, IV   B. I, II, V   C. II, III
    D. II, IV   E. II, III, V

35. WHICH economic situation is most readily solved with better functioning product and factor markets in terms of reducing imperfections and barriers to price competition?
    A. Hyperinflation   B. Repressed inflation
    C. Demand-pull inflation   D. Structural demand inflation
    E. Cost-push inflation

36. When a nation devalues its currency, it hopes to
    A. *increase* exports
    B. *increase* imports
    C. *affect* the price of gold
    D. *increase* its purchasing power
    E. *raise* the general price level

36._____

37. *WHICH* of the following are arguments in favor of a flexible exchange rate? It
    I. *allows* nations to hold the exchange rates stable and to help others to do so
    II. *frees* governments from having to hold huge amounts of foreign currencies to finance deficits
    III. *does not require* trade restrictions to curtail the net outflow of gold
    IV. *eliminates* speculative movements of capital before and after devaluation
    V. *does not add* to the uncertainty factor in business
    The *CORRECT* answer is:
    A. I, V   B. I, IV, V   C. II, III, IV
    D. II, IV   E. III, V

37._____

38. The monetarist or traditional approach contends that the stock of money and changes in it cause
    A. a state of full employment
    B. the shocks in the American economy
    C. built-in stabilizers to operate automatically
    D. optimism in the business and financial communities
    E. short-term stabilization

38._____

39. *WHY* is a counter-inflationary monetary policy *LESS DESIRABLE* than a restrictive fiscal policy? It
    A. results in a greater likelihood that the liquidity trap will occur
    B. may generate pessimism in the business and financial communities
    C. affects the marginal propensity to consume
    D. results in a cutback of government expenditures
    E. stifles one or two industries in order to cure the entire economy

39._____

40. *WHAT* is the aim of the fiscal policy of cutting back taxes during a recession? To
    A. *increase* the budgetary deficit
    B. *balance* the budget
    C. *restore* full employment to the economy
    D. *increase* consumption
    E. *increase* the reserves of commercial banks

40._____

41. All of the following are components of "near money" EXCEPT
    A. U.S. bonds
    B. short-term debt
    C. the cash value of insurance policies
    D. time deposits
    E. demand deposits

41._____

42. WHICH of the following are built-in stabilizers in   42.____
    the economy?
     I. Unemployment insurance payments
    II. Open market operations
   III. Private pensions and social security benefits
    IV. Tax reductions
     V. Dividend payments to stockholders
    The CORRECT answer is:
       A. I, II, III   B. I, III   C. I, III, V
       D. II, IV   E. I, III, IV

43. WHAT causes cost-push inflation?   43.____
       A. Technological advances which trigger a business boom
       B. Full employment
       C. Firms raising prices to counter rising costs
       D. Government stockpiles of materials
       E. Some components of the prime index rise while others
          remain stationary

44. WHICH of the following are VALID arguments against   44.____
    opponents to a federal debt?
     I. Businesses finance themselves through debt
    II. The overwhelming portion of the debt is of recent
         origin
   III. Stabilization policies imply deficits, planned
         balances, or surpluses
    IV. Most of the federal debt is held by foreigners
     V. More capital investment in the present leads to
         higher output in the future
    The CORRECT answer is:
       A. I, III, IV   B. II, V   C. I, III, V
       D. III, IV   E. I, II, V

45. WHAT is the main disadvantage of the stabilization   45.____
    policy of "formula flexibility"? It
       A. cannot guarantee a state of full employment
       B. can overreact to the economic cycles and accelerate
          or decelerate the stock of money erroneously
       C. sets artificial boundaries for the rate of increase
          of the money stock
       D. leads to automatic increases or reductions of tax rates
          which are, sometimes, based on an index reflecting
          changes in irrelevant factors
       E. depends on legislation that may be enacted too late
          or which may be completely absent

46. WHAT does a "balance of payments deficit" refer to ?   46.____
       A. A transaction that requires foreign currency
       B. A transaction that increases the supply of
          foreign currency
       C. An account indicating American imports exceed exports
       D. A situation where returns on capital abroad are
          higher than in the United States
       E. The balance of payments without the balancing items

47. *WHAT* was the MAIN contribution John Maynard Keynes made   47.____
    to economics? His
    A. understanding of aggregate demand
    B. criticism of classical and neo-classical economists
    C. theory of how a modern economic system operates
    D. ability to demonstrate the self-correcting mechanisms
       in the economy
    E. application of laissez-faire to modern economic theory

48. *WHAT* is "hard currency"? Money that   48.____
    A.   is acceptable to other countries in inter-
          national exchanges between them
    B.   is backed by gold
    C.   is full-bodied
    D.   cannot be devalued
    E.   is loaned by the International Monetary Fund

49. *WHAT* is the result of the condition in which the economy   49.____
    suffers from a "fiscal drag"?
    A. There has been a secular decline in the ratio of
       federal debt to GNP
    B. The percentage in tax collection exceeds the per-
       centage growth of the GNP
    C. The price index falls below a certain critical point
    D. Economic instability is aggravated by the lag of
       legislative action
    E. Decelerations in the stock of money cause downswings
       in economic activities

50. A tight money policy *PARTICULARLY* discriminates against   50.____
    A. investment in residential construction
    B. investment in the business community
    C. long-term loans
    D. government expenditures
    E. firms competing with households

KEY (CORRECT ANSWERS)

1. E	11. B	21. C	31. D	41. E
2. C	12. E	22. D	32. A	42. C
3. C	13. C	23. C	33. D	43. C
4. D	14. D	24. A	34. D	44. C
5. C	15. B	25. A	35. E	45. D
6. A	16. D	26. D	36. A	46. E
7. A	17. D	27. D	37. C	47. C
8. D	18. E	28. A	38. B	48. A
9. C	19. A	29. C	39. E	49. B
10. B	20. C	30. B	40. D	50. A

EXAMINATION SECTION

DIRECTIONS: Each question or incomplete statement is followed by several suggested answers or completions. Select the one that BEST answers the question or completes the statement. *PRINT THE LETTER OF THE CORRECT ANSWER IN THE SPACE AT THE RIGHT.*

1. *HOW DOES* a country solve a balance-of-payments deficit under a Pegged Exchange Rate System? By
   I. *borrowing* from the International Monetary Fund
   II. *floating* long-term securities
   III. *raising* the price of foreign currency
   IV. *changing* the exchange rate in the market
   V. *converting* domestic securities into investment in all kinds of foreign securities
   The *CORRECT* answer is:
   A. I, II, IV   B. I, III   C. I, IV
   D. I, III, IV   E. I, IV, V

2. *WHAT* is the purpose of a Price Index? It
   A. *indicates* price changes in any one given year
   B. *lists* the prices of goods and services in any one given year
   C. *summarizes* the average price of a group of goods and services in a onetime period relative to another
   D. *measures* the current dollar value of the GNP
   E. *points up* inflationary and recessionary tendencies within the economy

3. *WHICH* of the following BEST explains the growth of production in the United States?
   A. Growth of the population
   B. Increases in the factors of production
   C. Increases in the average educational levels of the labor force
   D. Increases in the supply of money
   E. Technological change

4. *WHICH* of the following are determinants of the demand for capital by business? The
   I. present amount of money held by the firm
   II. expected stream of future income
   III. price of capital goods
   IV. current rate of interest
   V. present indebtedness
   The *CORRECT* answer is:
   A. I, III, V   B. II, III, IV   C. I, IV, V
   D. II, IV, V   E. All of the above

5. *WHAT* is the MOST unstable component of aggregate demand? _____ demand.
   A. Consumption   B. Investment   C. Induced
   D. Government   E. Export

6. WHAT causes reduction in purchasing power of income or   6.____
   wealth during an inflation?
   A. Constant salaries
   B. Increase in prices
   C. Increase in unemployment
   D. Increase in price per unit of a product
   E. Decrease in disposable income

7. All of the following are TRUE of the Price System EXCEPT: 7.____
   It
   A. leads to an efficient allocation of resources
   B. leads to an unequal distribution of income
   C. ensures continued employment of labor and other
      resources
   D. allows firms to grow large enough to restrict output
      and raise prices
   E. reveals that prices often reflect only private rather
      than social costs and benefits

8. WHICH of the following are included in this year's GNP? A   8.____
     I. car manufactured this year but not yet sold
    II. car manufactured and sold this year
   III. car manufactured last year and sold this year
    IV. used car sold this year
     V. used car that is rebuilt and painted this year
   The CORRECT answer is:
   A. I, II   B. I, II, V   C. II, III, IV
   D. II, III, IV, V   E. All of the above

9. A marginal propensity to consume of 0.60 indicates that   9.____
   A. a household will consume 0.40 of any decrease in
      its level of disposable income
   B. a household will consume 0.40 regardless of the level
      of disposable income
   C. a household consumes 0.60 of its level of disposable
      income
   D. a household will consume 0.60 of any increase in its
      level of disposable income
   E. None of the above

10. Inflationary pressures are relieved by   10.____
    A. an increase in taxes
    B. an increase in taxes and government spending
    C. a decrease in taxes
    D. a decrease in taxes and government spending
    E. reducing the public debt

11. WHAT is the aim of the United States' economic policy?   11.____
    To eliminate _____ unemployment.
       A. frictional   B. cyclical   D. structural
       D. seasonal   E. all

12. A variation in business or economic activity which takes   12.____
    place within a one-year period, describes
       A. a secular trend   B. a business cycle
       C. a seasonal fluctuation   D. creeping inflation
       E. cost-push inflation

13. All of the following are *PRINCIPAL* Summary National
    Income Accounts except
    A. National Income
    B. Gross National Product
    C. Gross Investment
    D. Net National Product
    E. Personal Income

14. *WHICH* of the following are functions of money?
    I. medium of exchange
    II. commodity standard
    III. standard of value
    IV. determinant of price levels
    V. store of value
    The *CORRECT* answer is:
    A. I, II
    B. I, III, V
    C. I, II, III
    D. I, III, IV
    E. All of the above

15. In the rigid version of the Quantity Theory of Money, changes in
    A. velocity are proportional to changes in the money supply
    B. the nominal GNP are proportional to changes in the money supply
    C. the nominal GNP are proportional to changes in velocity
    D. the price level are proportional to changes in the money supply
    E. the price level are controlled by the money supply

16. *WHY* do demand deposits account for over 90% of all money transactions in the United States? A demand deposit is
    A. a bearer instrument
    B. more convenient
    C. interest-bearing
    D. a safer way of holding money
    E. a more acceptable means of exchange

17. *WHY* will a commercial bank hold excess reserves? To
    I. maintain solvency
    II. meet unexpected currency demands
    III. satisfy possible reserve losses resulting from the transfer of deposits to competing commercial banks
    IV. anticipate the future loan demands of borrowers
    V. comply with requirements of the Federal Open Market Committee
    The *CORRECT* answer is:
    A. I, II, III
    B. I, II, V
    C. II, III, IV
    D. I, III, V
    E. All of the above

18. According to Monetarists, changes in the money supply
    A. shift the demand-for-money schedule
    B. have no effect on the quantity of money demanded
    C. have an effect only upon household spending
    D. have a highly variable effect upon the level of income
    E. have an effect upon consumption and investment spending

19. *WHAT* is the *KEY* element in the growth process of an economy? Increase in the
    A. quantity and quality of natural resources
    B. economy's population
    C. population's participation in the labor force
    D. quality of labor
    E. accumulation of capital

20. Measures used to restore equilibrium in the balance of payments can have the effect of
    A. promoting international liquidity
    B. aggravating an unemployment problem
    C. reducing gold supplies
    D. reducing international reserves
    E. lowering the interest rate

21. *WHICH* of the following are counted as part of the GNP?
    I. Wheat grown and sold by farmers
    II. Flour sold by the mill to bakers
    III. Bread produced by bakers and sold to supermarkets
    IV. Bread sold to the ultimate consumer
    V. Bread sold to commercial sandwich makers
    The *CORRECT* answer is:
    A. I, III, IV   B. I, II, III   C. III, IV, V
    D. IV, V   E. All of the above

22. What is "real GNP"?
    A. A measure of the volume of real goods and services produced independently of price changes
    B. The market value of all goods and services
    C. The measure of the aggregate productive performance of the economy
    D. The average price of goods and services in one time-period relative to another
    E. The total income earned in the society

23. *WHICH* of the following is(are) part of the productive process?
    I. Extraction of raw materials
    II. Manufacture of intermediate products
    III. Assembly of final goods
    IV. Wholesaling activities
    V. Retailing activities
    The *CORRECT* answer is:
    A. I, II, III   B. III *only*   C. I, III, V
    D. III, IV, V   E. All of the above

24. *WHAT* is the relationship among the components of production, income, and demand, in a demand model?
    A. Interdependent   B. Equal   C. Autonomous
    D. Dependent   E. Cumulative

25. Government demand depends *PRIMARILY* on
    A. the size of production
    B. the price of social capital
    C. the current rate of interest

D. military commitments abroad
E. how society's desire for public goods is represented in the political process

26. WHICH of the following equations is CORRECT? 26._____
    A. GNI = GNP   B. GNI ≠ GNP   C. GNI > GNP
    D. GNI < GNP   E. GNP - GNI = Production

27. WHICH of the following events will NOT cause the market 27._____
    demand curve to shift upward?
    A. Increase in the number of consumers
    B. Increase in consumers' income
    C. Prices of substitute commodities rise
    D. Prices of complementary commodities rise
    E. Consumers' taste for the commodity increase

28. HOW DOES Current Dollar GNP differ from Constant Dollar 28._____
    GNP?
    A. It measures GNP in current year prices
    B. It measures GNP in base year prices
    C. It measures GNP during the current year
    D. It measures GNP during a one-year period
    E. There is no difference

29. WHAT does Say's Law conclude about the employment of 29._____
    economic resources?
    A. Full employment of economic resources is the normal condition of a private enterprise system
    B. The goal of a private enterprise economy is full employment of economic resources
    C. Full employment of economic resources can never occur in a private enterprise economy
    D. Full employment of economic resources is dependent upon production in a private enterprise economy
    E. Full employment of economic resources will approach, but never equal, the production level of a private enterprise economy

30. WHICH of the following is an example of discretionary 30._____
    fiscal policy?
    A. Government welfare payments
    B. Employer pension plans
    C. Payment of unemployment insurance
    D. Automatic changes in gross tax receipts that result from the income tax structure
    E. Deliberate changes in the level of government spending and net tax receipts

31. The contraction phase of the business cycle is 31._____
    characterized by
    A. *falling* interest rates
    B. *falling* price levels
    C. *falling* unemployment levels
    D. *rising* interest rates
    E. *rising* economic activity

32. Frictional unemployment generally occurs
    A. in a government-controlled society
    B. in a changing, free society
    C. in an economy experiencing technological advance
    D. during periods of insufficient aggregate demand
    E. in industries that are highly unionized

33. *WHICH* of the following is TRUE during a recession? _____ are severely affected.
    A. Non-durable goods
    B. Capital goods
    C. Durable goods
    D. Non-durable and durable goods
    E. Capital and durable goods

34. *WHAT* is the relationship between Net Investment and Gross Investment?
    A. Net Investment equals Gross Investment less taxes
    B. Net Investment equals Gross Investment less depreciation
    C. Net Investment equals Gross Investment less savings
    D. Net Investment equals Gross Investment less payments to the factors of production
    E. Net Investment equals Gross Investment less consumption

35. *WHAT* is the M_1 definition of money in the USA?
      I. Paper currency
     II. Demand deposits
    III. Deposits at non-bank thrift institutions
     IV. Time deposits at commercial banks
      V. Savings deposits at commercial banks
    The *CORRECT* answer is:
    A. I, V   B. I, IV, V   C. I, II
    D. I, II, V   E. All of the above

36. *WHICH* of the following may be considered a monetary standard?
      I. Paper currency   II. Coins
    III. Gold   IV. Silver
      V. Government securities
    The *CORRECT* answer is:
    A. I, II, V   B. II, III, V   C. II, III, IV
    D. I, V   E. All of the above

37. *WHAT* are the commercial banks' *PRINCIPAL* sources of liquidity?
      I. Currency
     II. Deposits at the Federal Reserve
    III. Money-market instruments
     IV. Short-and long-term loans to customers
      V. Fixed income obligations
    The *CORRECT* answer is:
    A. I, II, III   B. I, II   C. II, III, V
    D. I, II, IV   E. All of the above

38. WHICH of the following is TRUE of the National Income   38._____
    Theory? It
    A. focuses upon the expansion of aggregate supply over
       time
    B. evaluates the effect of resource growth upon
       productive capacity
    C. evaluates the increase in individuals' standard of
       living
    D. evaluates the rate at which aggregate demand must
       increase to achieve maximum growth
    E. has as its objective the design of economic policies
       that will move the economy onto the production
       possibility curve

39. Classical economists restore equilibrium to the world   39._____
    market by relying on
    A. changes in the rate of exchange
    B. devaluation of currencies
    C. the foreign-trade multiplier
    D. absolutely flexible price levels
    E. changing interest rates

40. WHY are intermediate products NOT counted as part of the   40._____
    GNP? They
    A. are an insignificant part of total productive
       activity
    B. would overestimate productive activity
    C. are goods that never reach the ultimate consumer
    D. are not considered part of the market value of goods
       and services
    E. might become part of a final product

41. Capital, as a factor of production, includes   41._____
       I. stocks and bonds   II. currency
     III. machines   IV. buildings
       V. inventories
    The CORRECT answer is:
    A. I, II   B. I, III, IV, V   C. I, II, V
    D. III, IV, V   E. All of the above

42. WHAT is the MAIN problem in constructing a price index?   42._____
    A. Data is difficult to obtain
    B. Prices of some units have risen while those for
       others have fallen
    C. There is no set averaging procedure that takes into
       account the relative importance of goods and services
    D. The set of goods and services, to which the average
       price has to be compared at different times, is
       constantly changing
    E. Prices are a function of the economy at specific times
       and cannot easily be compared because of variations in
       the economy

43. *WHAT* is the difference between a consumption good and an investment good? The
    A. source of the demand for the good
    B. type of good
    C. durability of the good
    D. degree of demand for the good
    E. production factor of the good

43.____

44. *WHAT* determines the marginal efficiency of capital for business? The
    A. current rate of interest
    B. rate of depreciation
    C. income stream and the price of capital goods
    D. rate of interest and the price of capital goods
    E. opportunity cost

44.____

45. All of the following items determine consumption demand EXCEPT
    A. expected future income
    B. disposable income
    C. population
    D. recent standard of living
    E. interest rates

45.____

46. *WHERE* is the *REAL* impact of inflation? On the
    A. level of real income
    B. level of disposable income
    C. level of price increases
    D. distribution level of income
    E. value of money

46.____

47. A demand schedule shows the relationship between the quantity demanded of a commodity over a given period of time *AND* the
    A. taste of consumers
    B. money income of consumers
    C. price of related products
    D. price of the commodity
    E. supply available

47.____

48. *WHAT* is the *DISPOSABLE INCOME* of a person whose personal income is $15,000., with personal income taxes of $3200., consumption at $7500., interest and payments amounting to $280., and personal savings totaling $4020.?
    A. $15,000.   B. $11,520.   C. $4020.
    D. $11,800.   E. $4300.

48.____

49. *WHICH* of the following is NOT a component of aggregate spending?
    A. Gross private domestic investment
    B. Personal consumption expenditures
    C. Government transfers
    D. Government purchase of goods and services
    E. Net exports

49.____

50. The ratio of the change in saving to the change in disposable income is called the
    A. consumption function
    B. average propensity to save
    C. average propensity to consume
    D. marginal propensity to save
    E. marginal propensity to consume

50.____

KEY (CORRECT ANSWERS)

1. B	11. B	21. D	31. A	41. D
2. C	12. C	22. A	32. B	42. D
3. E	13. C	23. E	33. E	43. C
4. B	14. B	24. A	34. B	44. C
5. B	15. D	25. E	35. C	45. A
6. D	16. D	26. A	36. E	46. D
7. C	17. C	27. D	37. A	47. D
8. B	18. E	28. A	38. E	48. D
9. D	19. E	29. A	39. D	49. C
10. A	20. B	30. E	40. B	50. D

EXAMINATION SECTION

DIRECTIONS: Each question or incomplete statement is followed by several suggested answers or completions. Select the one that BEST answers the question or completes the statement. *PRINT THE LETTER OF THE CORRECT ANSWER IN THE SPACE AT THE RIGHT.*

1. What does the statement that the GNP rose between 1958 and 1969 by $485.0 billions, actually mean?
    A. The market value of final goods produced in 1969 was 108% greater than in 1958
    B. There were 108% more goods and services produced in 1969 than in 1958
    C. Society was 108% better off in 1969 than in 1958
    D. The market value of goods produced in 1969 was 108% greater than the market value of goods produced in 1958
    E. It means that market prices increased by 108% over the twelve-year period

1.____

2. *HOW* does GNP compare with GNI in a given year?
    A. GNP is always higher
    B. GNP is always lower
    C. GNP equals GNI
    D. GNP is GNI
    E. They cannot be compared without more data

2.____

3. *WHAT* determines disposable income?
    A. Savings
    B. Production
    C. Income
    D. Interest rates
    E. Demand

3.____

4. The demand of businesses for new capital that does NOT include new capital replacing depreciated capital, is called _____ investment.
    A. opportunity
    B. capital
    C. optimum
    D. gross
    E. net

4.____

5. *WHICH* of the following are examples of non-durable goods demanded by households?
    I. Sporting equipment
    II. Clothing
    III. Transportation
    IV. Food and beverages
    V. Water
    The *CORRECT* answer is:
    A. I, II
    B. I, IV, V
    C. III, V
    D. II, IV
    E. IV, V

5.____

6. Demand-pull inflation develops when economic resources are fully employed *AND* there is a(n)
    I. increase in aggregate demand
    II. rise in business taxes which results in higher costs
    III. shortage of specific labor skills or supplies prior to full employment
    IV. surplus of materials which raises prices that are passed on to the consumer
    V. aggregate demand which grows at a faster rate than aggregate supply
    The *CORRECT* answer is:
    A. I, V
    B. I, III, V
    C. II, III, IV
    D. II, IV
    E. I, II, V

6.____

7. During a period of stable prices, one would expect
   A. high unemployment
   B. low unemployment
   C. greater aggregate demand
   D. lower aggregate demand
   E. economic equilibrium

8. WHICH of the following are examples of indirect business taxes?
   I. Excise taxes
   II. Sales taxes
   III. Business property taxes
   IV. Import duties
   V. License fees
   The CORRECT answer is:
   A. I, II
   B. II, IV
   C. I, III, V
   D. III, V
   E. All of the above

9. WHAT is the objective of changes in government spending and taxes? To
   A. balance the budget
   B. prevent inflations and recessions
   C. promote maximum employment, productivity, and purchasing power
   D. guarantee a basic standard of living to all citizens
   E. satisfy the public debt

10. When workers are between jobs or in the process of changing jobs, it is termed _____ unemployment.
    A. seasonal
    B. short-term
    C. structural
    D. frictional
    E. cyclical

11. What distinguishes hyperinflation from other forms of inflation?
    A. There is a reduction in the purchasing power of a unit of money
    B. Real income and wealth are affected
    C. The results are not shared equally by all economic groups
    D. There are annual increases in the general price level
    E. There is no dependable monetary system available to facilitate exchange

12. WHICH of the following is NOT included in the National Income?
    A. Wages
    B. Rent
    C. Interest
    D. Depreciation
    E. Profit

13. When money serves as a standard of value, it is akin to
    I. the speed of sound and light
    II. the value of gold and silver
    III. the weight and size of objects
    IV. the calories found in foods
    V. liquid assets
    The CORRECT answer is:
    A. I, IV
    B. II, V
    C. I, III, IV
    D. I, III, IV, V
    E. All of the above

14. WHICH of the following represent a Monetarist viewpoint?   14._____
    I. Money is unique
    II. The demand for money is sensitive to the rate of interest
    III. The velocity of money is variable
    IV. Fiscal measures result in only a small net change in the level of income
    V. Discretionary monetary management is a stabilizing factor in the economy
    The CORRECT answer is:
       A. I, IV, V   B. II, III, IV   C. I, II, IV
       D. II, III, V   E. II, III, IV, V

15. WHICH of the following is not a MAJOR source of increased   15._____
    productive capacity?
       A. The quantity and quality of natural resources
       B. An increase in the population's participation in the labor force
       C. An increase in the number of hours worked by the labor force
       D. An increase in the accumulation of capital
       E. Advances in technology

16. Why does the current IMF system perpetuate balance-of-   16._____
    payment maladjustments? Because of
       A. inflexible price levels
       B. economic goals of modern countries in full employment
       C. the inflexible exchange rate
       D. ill-defined terms of trade
       E. speculations in foreign currencies

17. Production in the United States economy does NOT include   17._____
    I. illegal goods
    II. services of housewives
    III. householders owning their own homes
    IV. the value of food produced and consumed on farms
    V. the value of food produced and consumed by household gardeners
    The CORRECT answer is:
       A. I, II   B. I, II, V   C. II, III, V
       D. I, II, III, V   E. All of the above

18. WHAT does the future stream of income for businesses   18._____
    depend on? Expected
    I. levels of future demand
    II. cost reductions from using capital
    III. levels of production
    IV. levels of investment
    V. technological change
    The CORRECT answer is:
       A. I, III, IV   B. I, IV, V   C. I, III
       D. I, II, V   E. I, III, IV, V

19. Aggregate demand is equal to the sum of all of the   19._____
    following demands EXCEPT
       A. consumption   B. investment   C. government
       D. export   E. import

20. The amount of wages, interest, and rent required to hire   20.____
    one unit of labor, capital, or land is called the
       A. real output   B. price mechanism
       C. factor price   D. production price
       E. substitution effect

21. WHICH of the following is a CORRECT assumption based   21.____
    on Say's Law? Individuals
       A. work to satisfy non-economic desires
       B. work to buy goods and services
       C. work to create and add to a "nest-egg"
       D. consume beyond their disposable income
       E. consume at a rate equal to their disposable income

22. HOW can an inflationary gap be eliminated? By   22.____
       A. an increase in government spending and a decrease
          in net tax revenues
       B. equal decreases in net tax revenues and government
          spending
       C. equal increases in net tax revenues and government
          spending
       D. decreases in net tax revenues
       E. an increase in net tax revenues and a decrease in
          transfer payments

23. WHAT does the "Potential GNP" measure?   23.____
       A. How much could be produced when land, labor, and
          capital are fully utilized
       B. Next year's output based on economic trends in-
          dicated by this year's GNP
       C. Output at full employment
       D. Output when 100% of the civilian labor force is
          employed
       E. Output when the economy is at equilibrium

24. An expansion period in the business cycle is characterized 24.____
    by increases in
       I. employment   II. prices   III. money supply
      IV. interest   V. profits
    The CORRECT answer is:
       A. I, III   B. II, III, V   C. I, III
       D. I, II, III, V   E. All of the above

25. The average number of times a unit of money is used   25.____
    during the year to purchase final goods and services,
    is called the
       A. rate of exchange   B. store of value
       C. velocity of money   D. common denominator
       E. demand factor

26. When a country adopts a commodity standard, the money supply depends upon the
    I. promissory notes issued by the government
    II. aggregate demand for the chosen commodity
    III. defined commodity content of the paper currency
    IV. available quantity of the chosen commodity
    V. commercial use of the commodity
    The CORRECT answer is:
    A. I, II, III
    B. II, III, IV, V
    C. I, II, III, IV
    D. III, IV, V
    E. III, IV

27. All of the following are TRUE of the Monetarists EXCEPT:
    A. Monetarists favor stable monetary growth rather than discretionary monetary management
    B. Monetarists view monetary policy as a means to achieving a more efficient allocation of resources
    C. Monetarists contend that monetary policy is predictable due to the sensitivity of velocity to the rate of interest
    D. Monetarists contend that monetary policy crowds out private investment
    E. Monetarists contend that velocity is predictable

28. An economy's poverty level is relative to the economy's
    A. resources
    B. capital
    C. population growth
    D. standard of living
    E. per capita output

29. All of the following are changes in the structure of the economy which guarantee a higher degree of stability EXCEPT:
    A. The flow of government expenditures is stable
    B. Disposable personal income fluctuations are reduced
    C. Deposits in banks are federally insured
    D. The Federal Reserve System prevents the collapse of banks
    E. The public has greater confidence in the economy

30. The level of production tends to adjust to
    A. price levels
    B. the factors of production available
    C. the level of aggregate demand
    D. the highest profit margin
    E. the rate of production

31. When should a product be demanded by the government? When
    A. it benefits the public sector
    B. its value outweighs its cost
    C. it benefits the private sector
    D. it ensures production of goods
    E. the interest rate declines

32. WHAT is the largest component of aggregate demand? _____ demand.
    A. Consumption
    B. Investment
    C. Induced
    D. Government
    E. Export

33. *WHAT* is wealth?
    A. The assets that result from economic activity
    B. An accumulated stock of material assets
    C. Income minus expenditures
    D. Resources
    E. Anything of market value

34. *WHICH* of the following does NOT cause an increase in supply? A(n)
    A. increase in the number of producers of the commodity
    B. reduction in the price of other commodities related in production
    C. reduction in factor prices
    D. improvement in technology
    E. increase in the commodity price

35. The business sector's ability to produce does NOT depend on
    A. the quantity of economic resources supplied by the household sector
    B. the quantity of labor units
    C. the amount of capital available
    D. natural resources
    E. the ability to sell output

36. *WHICH* of the following is TRUE of the public debt? It
    A. burdens future generations
    B. eventually will lead to Federal bankruptcy
    C. aggravates inflationary and recessionary tendencies
    D. burdens individuals who elect to save and not consume
    E. burdens individuals who elect to consume and not save

37. The Accelerator Theory is used to explain
    A. the business cycle
    B. how changes in investment affect the business cycle
    C. fluctuations in capital stock and the level of inventory investment
    D. fluctuations in capital stock and technological change
    E. fluctuations in inventories over the business cycle

38. According to the Acceleration Principle, net investment is a constant sum each year when sales
    A. volume decreases
    B. volume remains constant
    C. increase by a decreasing sum each year
    D. increase by a constant sum each year
    E. increase at a constant rate each year

39. *WHY* are financial assets, other than money, NOT accepted as a medium of exchange?
    A. They are not safe
    B. They lose nominal value when converted into money
    C. They do not have a fixed nominal value
    D. They must first be converted into money
    E. They are not readily converted into money

40. The Federal Reserve System consists of
     I. a Board of Governors
    II. a Monetary Fund Committee
   III. Member commercial banks
    IV. Member Savings and Loan Associations
     V. District Federal Reserve Banks
   The *CORRECT* answer is:
     A. I, II, V   B. I, III, V   C. I, II, III, V
     D. II, III, IV, V E. All of the above

41. According to the Phillips Curve, high unemployment rates are associated with
     A. low rates of inflation   B. high rates of inflation
     C. large increases in wages D. small increases in wages
     E. low productive rates

42. All of the following are objections to economic growth EXCEPT: It
     A. pollutes the atmosphere
     B. does not resolve socio-economic problems
     C. eliminates the need for substitute goods
     D. wastes economic resources
     E. leads to man's enslavement by technology

43. *WHEN* is income in equilibrium? When
     A. consumption and saving are equal
     B. consumption and disposable income are equal
     C. intended investment and savings are equal
     D. all disposable income is consumed
     E. the marginal propensity to save is equal to the marginal propensity to consume

44. The aggregate demand for goods and services produced in the economy equals total demand
     A. *less* autonomous demand   B. *plus* export demand
     C. *less* export demand   D. *plus* import demand
     E. *less* import demand

45. *WHAT* is the average propensity to save for an individual whose yearly disposable income is $10,000. and consumption is $9200.?
     A. 0.80   B. 1.08   C. 0.92   D. 0.08   E. 0.90

46. *WHAT* is Cyclical Unemployment? Unemployment
     A. caused by insufficient aggregate demand
     B. due to changes in demand for particular products
     C. caused by technological advance
     D. due to workers being temporarily out of work
     E. due to workers voluntarily leaving the job market

47. *WHAT* category of unemployment describes a worker who lacks the skills needed to qualify for available job openings? _____ unemployment.
     A. Frictional   B. Productive   C. Structural
     D. Cyclical   E. Linear

48. An inconvertible paper standard consists of a money supply that 48.____
    A. is backed by gold
    B. is backed by gold but is not convertible into gold
    C. is backed by a specific commodity but is not convertible into that commodity
    D. includes only the debts of commercial banks which have gold backing
    E. includes the debts of the government and/or commercial banks

49. The number of district Federal Reserve Banks is 49.____
    A. 6   B. 12   C. 18   D. 24   E. 36

50. Keynesian Theory emphasizes the use of 50.____
    A. monetary policy   B. fiscal policy
    C. open market valuations   D. selective credit controls
    E. reserve requirements

KEY (CORRECT ANSWERS)

1. D	11. E	21. B	31. B	41. A
2. C	12. D	22. B	32. A	42. C
3. B	13. C	23. C	33. B	43. C
4. E	14. C	24. E	34. E	44. E
5. D	15. A	25. C	35. E	45. D
6. B	16. C	26. D	36. D	46. A
7. A	17. B	27. D	37. E	47. C
8. E	18. D	28. D	38. D	48. E
9. C	19. E	29. D	39. D	49. B
10. D	20. C	30. C	40. B	50. B

ANSWER SHEET

TEST NO. _____ PART _____ TITLE OF POSITION _____
(AS GIVEN IN EXAMINATION ANNOUNCEMENT - INCLUDE OPTION, IF ANY)

PLACE OF EXAMINATION _____ (CITY OR TOWN) _____ (STATE) _____ DATE _____ RATING _____

USE THE SPECIAL PENCIL. MAKE GLOSSY BLACK MARKS.

Make only ONE mark for each answer. Additional and stray marks may be counted as mistakes. In making corrections, erase errors COMPLETELY.

ANSWER SHEET

TEST NO. ____________ PART ______ TITLE OF POSITION ______________________________
(AS GIVEN IN EXAMINATION ANNOUNCEMENT - INCLUDE OPTION, IF ANY)

PLACE OF EXAMINATION ______________________________ DATE ______________
(CITY OR TOWN) (STATE)

RATING

USE THE SPECIAL PENCIL. MAKE GLOSSY BLACK MARKS.

1 A B C D E	26 A B C D E	51 A B C D E	76 A B C D E	101 A B C D E
2 A B C D E	27 A B C D E	52 A B C D E	77 A B C D E	102 A B C D E
3 A B C D E	28 A B C D E	53 A B C D E	78 A B C D E	103 A B C D E
4 A B C D E	29 A B C D E	54 A B C D E	79 A B C D E	104 A B C D E
5 A B C D E	30 A B C D E	55 A B C D E	80 A B C D E	105 A B C D E
6 A B C D E	31 A B C D E	56 A B C D E	81 A B C D E	106 A B C D E
7 A B C D E	32 A B C D E	57 A B C D E	82 A B C D E	107 A B C D E
8 A B C D E	33 A B C D E	58 A B C D E	83 A B C D E	108 A B C D E
9 A B C D E	34 A B C D E	59 A B C D E	84 A B C D E	109 A B C D E
10 A B C D E	35 A B C D E	60 A B C D E	85 A B C D E	110 A B C D E

Make only ONE mark for each answer. Additional and stray marks may be counted as mistakes. In making corrections, erase errors COMPLETELY.

11 A B C D E	36 A B C D E	61 A B C D E	86 A B C D E	111 A B C D E
12 A B C D E	37 A B C D E	62 A B C D E	87 A B C D E	112 A B C D E
13 A B C D E	38 A B C D E	63 A B C D E	88 A B C D E	113 A B C D E
14 A B C D E	39 A B C D E	64 A B C D E	89 A B C D E	114 A B C D E
15 A B C D E	40 A B C D E	65 A B C D E	90 A B C D E	115 A B C D E
16 A B C D E	41 A B C D E	66 A B C D E	91 A B C D E	116 A B C D E
17 A B C D E	42 A B C D E	67 A B C D E	92 A B C D E	117 A B C D E
18 A B C D E	43 A B C D E	68 A B C D E	93 A B C D E	118 A B C D E
19 A B C D E	44 A B C D E	69 A B C D E	94 A B C D E	119 A B C D E
20 A B C D E	45 A B C D E	70 A B C D E	95 A B C D E	120 A B C D E
21 A B C D E	46 A B C D E	71 A B C D E	96 A B C D E	121 A B C D E
22 A B C D E	47 A B C D E	72 A B C D E	97 A B C D E	122 A B C D E
23 A B C D E	48 A B C D E	73 A B C D E	98 A B C D E	123 A B C D E
24 A B C D E	49 A B C D E	74 A B C D E	99 A B C D E	124 A B C D E
25 A B C D E	50 A B C D E	75 A B C D E	100 A B C D E	125 A B C D E